Weird and Wicked Winchcombe

Second edition 2015

Acknowledgements
Many thanks to David Crow, Barbara Edward, Carol Harris and Alastair Robinson for their invaluable help in my research

ISBN: 978-0-9562328-7-8

Weird and Wicked Winchcombe

The Darker Side of the Town's History

Anne Crow *(a museum volunteer)*

All profits from this publication will go to
Winchcombe Folk and Police Museum,
part of The Winchcombe Town Trust,
registered charity no. 234734.

INTRODUCTION

Winchcombe is a picturesque Cotswold town with a rich history. In prehistoric times, Stone Age man built one of the finest surviving long barrows with drystone retaining walls, stone-lined burial chambers and a clever false entrance. The Romans seem to have had a farmstead at Almsbury, close to the town centre, and they left beautiful mosaic floors in Spoonley Wood and Wadfield Villas, at some time between A.D. 100 and 400. At the beginning of the Ninth Century, Winchcombe was a centre of Mercian royal estate management, and there was almost definitely a palace here, probably at the east end of Abbey Terrace. The town was defended by a castle to the south of St Peter's Church. For a time in the Eleventh Century, Winchcombe was even the capital of its own county.

Winchcombe Abbey was founded at the end of the Eighth Century, and rebuilt in the Twelfth Century. Under Richard Kidderminster, it was a distinguished centre of learning. Although it was totally demolished in 1539 when Henry VIII ordered the dissolution of the monasteries, stones from the Abbey can still be seen around the town and in the Museum. Two stone coffins, excavated from the site of the Abbey Church, are kept in St Peter's Church, as well as some decorated tiles and a door.

For centuries Winchcombe prospered because pilgrims flocked to St. Kenelm's shrine and nearby Hailes Abbey. Several members of the royal family also visited Winchcombe in Tudor times, and Queen Elizabeth even granted Winchcombe a Royal Charter to help it recover from the dissolution of the Abbey. Catherine Parr, last wife of Henry VIII, married Sir Thomas Seymour and lived and died here.

The history of the town has a darker side, however. In her ***Annals of Winchcombe and Sudeley***, written in 1877, Emma Dent records that the Vikings sacked Winchcombe Abbey. She also writes that, during the civil war in the Twelfth Century between Stephen and Matilda, Milo, Constable of Gloucester *"assaulted Winchcombe, burnt the greatest part of the place, and carried off those whom he had robbed"* (p. 79). When Henry VIII dissolved the Abbey, pilgrims stopped coming. From then on, life for many of the residents of Winchcombe was a constant struggle, leading to an increase in the crimes associated with poverty such as poaching, theft, begging, vagrancy and drunkenness.

This book picks out just a few stories of the darker incidents in Winchcombe's history - some tragedies, some crimes and punishments, as well as strange stories of witches, wizards, ghosts.

Eliza Fawdry, murdered by her husband the day after the wedding, is buried here, in St Peter's churchyard, in the grave of her grandparents, Mr and Mrs Day.

CONTENTS

St. Kenelm Miracle Play, performed the Sunday after his Saint's Day, July 17th

Askebert cuts off Kenelm's head in the St. Kenelm miracle play

LIST OF ILLUSTRATIONS

The Wicked and the Woeful:

Crimes and Punishments

Winchcombe stocks at the Old Town Hall

FRATRICIDE

Saint Kenelm

According to legend, the wicked Quenthryth, daughter of King Kenulf, plotted to have her seven year old brother, Kenelm, murdered because she wanted the throne of Mercia for herself. Supposedly, by offering Askebert, her brother's tutor and guardian, money as well as her body, she persuaded him to kill the little boy on a hunting trip to the Clent Hills. Before the hunt, Kenelm dreamed of climbing a tall tree and then watching, as his dearest friend chopped it down. Frightened, he asked his nurse to interpret it for him, and she realised that the dream signified that someone was plotting to kill him. Young Kenelm ignored this warning, went on the hunt, had his head cut off by Askebert while he was asleep, and was buried in a wooded valley.

Years later, a poor widow and her white cow miraculously discovered the body, and a milk-white dove with golden wings soared up to heaven and took a scroll to Rome telling of the evil deed. It was dropped at the altar of St Peter's for Pope Silvester II to read. He was horrified and wrote to the Archbishop of Canterbury, who commissioned a party from Winchcombe, the capital of Mercia, to search for the grave. They saw a pillar of light shining over a thicket, and, when they dug there, they found Kenelm's body. As they removed the remains, a spring of health-giving water burst forth.

St Kenelm, above door to well-housing

The body was then carried towards Winchcombe. After an incident at Pyriford with a company from Worcester Abbey, who tried to prevent the remains leaving Worcestershire, the escort marched swiftly. Wherever they paused to rest, another spring miraculously appeared! Exhausted and thirsty, they stopped within sight of Winchcombe Abbey, and placed Kenelm's remains on the ground. In that exact spot, a final spring gushed forth to refresh them.

As they approached the Abbey, the bells rang out of their own accord! Quenthryth saw the procession from a window and attempted to read Psalm 53 (or 109) backwards, in order to curse the body and its escort. The crowd shouted, "Kenelm is truly God's martyr"; Quenthryth replied, "As truly as my eyes are resting on this psalter." At this, her two eyes burst from their sockets and fell *'plop'* on the pages of the open book. Thus was the murderess appropriately punished by divine intervention.

THE MURDERED KING CARRIED TO WINCHCOMBE.

The legend was much embellished in the Twelfth and Thirteenth Centuries, so there are various versions of the story. Probably the best known reference is in Chaucer's ***Canterbury Tales***, when the Nun's Priest told how Chanticleer, a cockerel, tried to persuade his wife, Pertelote, of the significance of his dream:

> *"Now, take St Kenelm's life which I've been reading;*
> *He was Kenulphus' son, the noble King*
> *Of Mercia. Now, St Kenelm dreamt a thing*
> *Shortly before they murdered him one day.*
> *He saw his murder in a dream, I say.*
> *His nurse expounded it and gave her reasons*
> *On every point and warned him against treasons,*
> *But, as the saint was only seven years old,*
> *All that she said about it left him cold.*
> *He was so holy, how could visions hurt?*
> *By God, I willingly would give my shirt*
> *To have you read his legend as I've read it;"*

In the Sixteenth Century, a Chapel was built by the well which sprang up on the Sudeley estate, and a conduit built over the well. This chapel was destroyed in 1830, but a new well-housing was built in 1887, in honour of Queen Victoria's Golden Jubilee. That still stands, and travellers can refresh themselves at his well. However, the well-housing is usually locked, although it is opened for the festival of St Kenelm, July 17th. Every year his well is blessed by the church, and his story is told in a Miracle Play, acted out at the site of Saint Kenelm's Well.

Post Script:

Not surprisingly there is very little truth in the legend. It is estimated that Kenelm was about 36 when he died in 811 or 812, and his sister, Quenthryth, was later appointed Abbess of Minster-in-Thanet, Reculver and Southminster, and doubtless she would have been Abbess of Winchcombe, a double house founded by her father. A woman could never have assumed the throne in the Ninth Century, so the more likely murderer was Ceolwulf, Kenulf's younger brother. Kenulf did not appoint his brother as heir, suggesting that he did not trust him. Strangely, Ceolwulf was not consecrated for some months after Kenulf's death; then he was driven from power within a few months.

Winchcombe Abbey prospered, as the legend attracted many pilgrims to the Abbey Church where Saint Kenelm was buried. In the Twelfth Century, William of Malmesbury wrote that: *"There is hardly any place in England more venerated, or where greater numbers of people attend at the festival; and this arises from the long continued belief in his sanctity and the frequent exhibition of miracles."*

When the site of Winchcombe Abbey was extensively excavated in 1815, a small stone coffin was found next to a larger coffin. The smaller one contained a child's skull and other bones, as well as a knife with a very long bade. This was witnessed by Edmund Thomas Browne, High Bailiff of Winchcombe, who also recorded the conclusion of *'a celebrated antiquary'* that the coffins were those of King Kenulf and his son, Kenelm. The bones and knife disintegrated on contact with air, but the coffins can be seen in St. Peter's Church. Could it be that the monks deliberately planted a body and a murder weapon to authenticate the legend and attract more pilgrims?

In ***The Winchcombe and Sudeley Record,*** of September, 1891, Emma Dent expresses her opinion that, *"We smile at the absurdity of the legend, and wonder how those clever monks had the audacity to canonize the murdered child, not only imputing miraculous power to his dead body, but also to the spring itself."*

TREACHERY

Eadric the Grasper

Eadric Streona ('the grasper') was Ealdorman of Mercia from 1007 to 1017. He was married to Edgith, daughter of King Æthelred the Unready, but he betrayed his father-in-law and his people to side with the Viking invaders.

Eadric has gone down in history as the greatest traitor of Anglo-Saxon times:

"For ... there was one Eadric, a man infamously skilled in such transactions, whom the king had made governor of the Mercians. This fellow was the refuse of mankind, the reproach of the English; an abandoned glutton, a cunning miscreant, who had become opulent, not by nobility, but by specious language and impudence. This artful dissembler, capable of feigning anything, was accustomed, by pretended fidelity, to scent out the king's designs, that he might treacherously divulge them. Often, when dispatched to the enemy as a mediator of peace, he inflamed them to battle. His perfidy was sufficiently conspicuous in this king's reign, but much more so in the next."

William of Malmesbury's
Chronicles of the Kings of England,
Chapter X, A.D. 979 - 1017

Æthelred the Unready, Saxon King of England, 978-1013, 1014-1016 A.D.

John of Worcester wrote about one of his betrayals:
"The crafty and treacherous Eadric Streona, plotting to deceive the noble Ealdorman Ælfhelm, prepared a great feast for him at Shrewsbury at which, when he came as a guest, Eadric greeted him as if he were an intimate friend. But on the third or fourth day of the feast, when an ambush had been prepared, he took him into the wood to hunt. When all were busy with the hunt, one Godwine Porthund, a Shrewsbury butcher, whom Eadric had dazzled long before with great gifts and many promises so that he might perpetrate the crime, suddenly leapt out from the ambush, and execrably slew the Ealdorman Ælfhelm."

In 1015, together with 40 ships and their crews, Eadric Streona deserted Æthelred as he lay dying, and joined forces with Canute, the Danish invader, to fight against Æthelred's son, Edmund Ironside. When at length peace was made, Canute restored to Eadric the Earldom of Mercia. Canute, however, did not trust him and had him slain on Christmas Day, 1017.

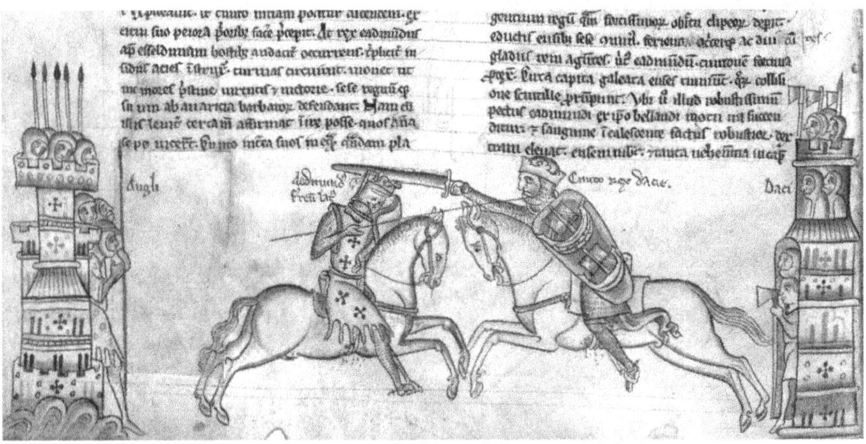

Edmund Ironside (left) and Canute (right)

Eadric is of great significance in the history of Winchcombe because, in 1017, he abolished the county of Winchcombeshire and incorporated it into Gloucestershire. It seems he may have had a grudge against the shire, probably because the nobles of that county were supporters of Edmund.

Emma Dent tells of this in her ***Annals:***

"When Canute obtained the crown of England, A.D. 1017, the government of Mercia was given to Edric Streona. Up to this time, Winchcombe had enjoyed the distinction of being a county and sheriffdom in itself, a distinction which doubtless was conferred upon it for its commanding position and its containing a royal residence. While Edric was governor, Winchcombe was deprived of her high honours, and was incorporated with the county of Gloucester, and placed under the same jurisdiction.

This union was of course highly advantageous both to Winchcombe and the county; though it is easy to imagine the feelings of discontent which pervaded the loyal hearts of the Winchcombites when they found themselves deprived of their distinguished position, and figuratively reduced to a level with their neighbours, for it is recorded that Gloucester had been deprived of its title of "Cittie" a few years before, when Winchcombe boasted that of being the fairest in Mercia!

We can hardly give Edric Streona the credit, and we may be sure he had none at the time, for making this great change from any good motive – it was possibly to humiliate Winchcombe, 'the faire and chieffest cittie of Mercia,' and to take revenge on her loyal sons, who had always proved so true to the king !

The end of Edric Streona was worthy of his career. Canute ordered him to be slain in his palace, saying with irony, that as Edric wished to please him, so he would advance him higher than all the noblemen in England, and thereupon ordered his head to be cut off and placed on a pole on the highest gate in London, to be seen by all beholders. His body was ignominiously cast without the city walls." (pp. 60-61)

The monument in the Church of the Holy Cross, Avening
Underneath is the following inscription:-
"Here lyeth the body of Henry Brydges, Esquior, son to Lord Chavndos, Baron of Shevdley, who departed this life, the 24th day of Janvarii, Anno Dom. 1615"

HIGHWAY ROBBERY & PIRACY

Convicted highwaymen and pirates were usually hanged in a public place in order to deter others. However, Emma Dent, in ***The Annals of Winchcombe and Sudeley*** records that Henry Brydges, son of Sir John Brydges, first Lord Chandos of Sudeley, was a convicted highwayman and a privateer, and yet, in 1615, he died peacefully in his bed at the age of 81, having been given a pardon by King James I:

"Henry, the fourth son, who, according to his father's will, must have been left with very slender means, and having in those times of peace no vent for his love of adventure, ... is said to have followed the life of a freebooter, indulging in deeds of lawlessness and robbery almost surpassing our modern powers of belief. We can readily imagine how the almost impassable roads, thick woods, and broken ground of this neighbourhood must have aided the young nobleman in his first steps as a freebooter.

Startling to the inmates of the Castle must have been the first stories which reached them of plunder, and perhaps murder; and from time to time, as they came to the ears of Lord and Lady Chandos, painful indeed must have been their feelings when the horrible suspicion became a reality, that the daring young highwayman was none other than one of the youngest scions of their own house.

We find him afterwards living in Kent, attracted thither perhaps by a larger field for booty, or possibly having made his own neighbourhood too hot to hold him. He, however, eventually returned, and traditions of his maraudings still hang about the Gloucestershire village where he lies buried." (pp. 214-5)

Sudeley Castle, 1880, woodblock print drawn by A.F. Lydon

Gloucester Gaol

HANGINGS

Thomas Freeman

In April, 1788, Thomas Freeman, a Winchcombe man, aged 30, was hanged on the gallows at Over for housebreaking. He was taken to the gallows in a cart, sitting on his own coffin.

In 1811, William Townley was convicted of burglary and hanged on the new drop style gallows erected on the roof of Gloucester prison gatehouse.

William Townley

In ***Foul Deeds and Suspicious Deaths in the Cotswolds,*** Nell Darby tells that William Townley was born in Winchcombe in 1781 and christened in St Peter's Church. He and his older brother, John, were persistent offenders. When William was 17, they were caught and convicted of burglary. He was sent to the Penitentiary House for two years. In 1803, he was caught again and sentenced to transportation for seven years.

Instead of being sent to Australia, he was kept on one of the prison ships kept at Woolwich. This old warship had been used as a prison hulk since at least 1777. It was over-crowded, housing about 400 prisoners, who were kept in appalling conditions. They were chained, even when they were asleep, and kept in cramped cells. They were punished with floggings or by being kept in solitary confinement. They were made to work from early in the morning and were rarely taken out into the fresh air.

In 1806, he was pardoned, in return for agreeing to join the army, and he signed up for the Worcestershire militia as a substitute for someone who did not want to perform his obligation. He should have been paid forty guineas, but was only given an advance of ten. When he had spent this, he broke into the house of George Skinner, near Winchcombe, and stole a coat and two shirts, worth a total of seven shillings. He was caught and sent to Gloucester Gaol in October 1810. At the Lent Assizes, he was convicted of burglary and sentenced to be hanged on Saturday, March 23rd, 1811.

After leaving the court, the judge was travelling towards Hereford for the next assizes. En route, he was told some favourable things about Townley, and he decided to grant him a reprieve. Unfortunately, his letter was sent to Hereford instead of Gloucester by mistake.

When the error was discovered next morning, the letter was sent post haste to Gloucester, but it arrived too late. Tragically, William Townley had been hanging on the drop over the lodge for more than twenty minutes and could not be revived. He was buried in the churchyard in Winchcombe.

Chandos Grammar School, Chandos Street

A BRUTAL BEATING

In 1844, Winchcombe hit the headlines in the national press when Conrad Carter was brutally beaten by his schoolmaster, Charles Lapworth, at Chandos School and died some months later. The following report is taken from ***The Gloucester Chronicle*** (13:01:1844):

RUMOURED DEATH FROM ILL-TREATMENT

CENSURE ON A SCHOOLMASTER BY THE JURY

Great excitement has existed in Winchcomb, and the neighbourhood, during the past few days, from the circumstances attending the death of Conrad Algernon Carter, son of Giles Carter Esq., solicitor of that town. Deceased was between twelve and thirteen years of age, and his death occurred on the 29th ult. Reports having reached the ears of Mr Barnett, coroner of this district, that death had been accelerated by ill-treatment received by the lad while at school, that gentleman deemed it his duty to hold an inquest on the body, which took place accordingly on Saturday last, at the George Inn, Winchcomb, before a jury of 18 most respectable inhabitants of the town.

...

It was further given in evidence, that, on the occasion referred to, deceased came into the school rather late, and, on being asked the reason, said his father had employed him; that his master thereupon beat him with a cane in a very severe manner over the head, neck and arms; that during the chastisement the boy fell down, and on his threatening to tell his father the punishment was repeated; and that the deceased was so much hurt that he laid his head on the desk during the whole of the remainder of the school hours. it was stated further that, as he was leaning his head upon the desk, the master again came up to him, struck him over the head and shoulders with the cane, and on his falling down seized him by the waist and again inflicted unmerciful punishment upon him. One of the deceased's fellow-scholars deposed that, after the school was over, he asked the boy to show him where he had been beaten, and, on his taking off his coat and waistcoat and throwing back his shirt, the neck and under the arms were, to use the witness's expression, "red, green and back," and the skin on the left shoulder "reeved up", and they wiped the blood off with a pocket handkerchief.

...

He was taken by his mother the same evening and shown to the Rev. Mr Harvey and E.T. Brown, Esq., two of the trustees of the school, and Mr Newman, surgeon of Winchcombe. ... A post mortem examination was made by Mr Hawkins, surgeon of Cheltenham, who stated he found the body, particularly the neck, ulcerated to a very great extent, but that the immediate cause of death was ulceration of the lungs. Mr Hawkins said it was impossible to say what was the exciting cause of the disease, or whether it in any way originated in the punishment deceased was stated to have received at school.

...

The jury, after a short deliberation, returned a verdict, "That the deceased Conrad Algernon Carter died of disease of the lungs." But ..."The jurors cannot separate, after returning their verdict, without expressing their high sense of a disapprobation of the conduct of Mr Lapworth, the schoolmaster, towards the deceased in March last, when he inflicted an extent of corporal punishment on him which was unwarrantable, and done in a manner most discreditable.

The jurors also consider that, after the deceased was allowed by his parents to return to the school after the Midsummer holidays (although in bad health) on the earnest solicitation of others and under the full sanction of the school committee, and the particular wishes expressed by one of them (who appeared most desirous of restoring harmony and good feeling in the school) the orders then given by Mr Lapworth to the other boys not to associate with, or speak to the deceased, as before had been their habit during the years he had been at the Grammar School of Winchcombe, were imprudent, and injudicious in the extreme and by no means calculated to reconcile parent or child."

However, there emerged another side to this story. The School Trustees met to consider the matter and, in the record of their meeting, they noted that, the previous year (January 1843), the child *"had been guilty of insubordination on several occasions and that the committee resolved that, on a repetition of such conduct, the said Conrad Algernon Carter should be expelled and that they requested Mr Lapworth to furnish Mr Carter, the father, with a copy of the Resolution."*

The Trustees also examined the cane used and concluded that *"The instrument with which the chastisement was inflicted was a small cane the common size of a schoolmaster's cane being about two feet six inches long and three eighths of an inch in diameter, which cane was produced before them* (the Trustees) *in evidence against a report in circulation ... that the instrument with which the punishment was inflicted was one of a very different description having knobs in it and in every way improper to be used on such occasions."*

The Trustees concluded that *"although the punishment was severe, it could not in the remotest degree be connected with the malady of which Conrad Carter had died"*. The Trustees' report also states *"that it appears to them that the punishment, even admitting that expulsion was the alternative, was severe, but they feel confident that those who coincide with them in opinion, after hearing the evidence of Mr Newman and Mr Browne, will agree likewise with them that the sufferings Mr Lapworth has undergone from the charges against him by the jury on the inquest, and the stigma upon his character and reputation in his conduct as a schoolmaster, until this investigation took place, is a far more serious punishment than any, under the evidence before them, the Trustees would have felt themselves authorised to inflict, or which strict justice demanded."*

Charles Lapworth was exonerated and remained master of the school for another 22 years, until he died in 1866. A letter of support, signed by 27 of his former pupils, was published in the Cheltenham Examiner on January 24th, 1844:

"We the undersigned, having been scholars under your tuition, and having invariably received from you the most kind, generous and humane treatment, deem it our duty to express to you the high sense we entertain of your uniformly honourable and gentlemanly conduct, and the gratitude we feel towards you for your untiring and persevering exertions, whilst we were in your school, to confer upon us the blessing of a good education, of which exertions we shall feel the benefit throughout life.

We beg also further to state, during the time we were in the school, you never, in our estimation, flogged any boy in an improper or excessive manner, but behaved towards us all with that kind forbearance and good-will which now insures for you (after your duties towards us are at an end) a most heart-felt and cordial expression of our esteem and respect, unabated in the slightest degree, by the false and malignant aspersions attempted to be attached to your character."

TRANSPORTATION

In his '***Reminiscences***', (p. 23) John Oakey, born in 1847, wrote about a burglar who was heroically captured by one John Banning, a Winchcombe constable:

"In High Street, where Mr. H.W. Stephens' offices are, an old gentleman named Trotman lived, and during his life the house was burgled by a chimney sweep, David Johns, from Stow-on-the-Wold. He was not the best of characters, and on one occasion when a Winchcombe constable met him just past Hailes Abbey on his way home and challenged him, David (Johns) *immediately struck the constable with some heavy instrument and floored him. This was about midnight.*

Queen Anne House, H.W. Stephens' offices

They fought till morning, when they were found by a man going to work, both exhausted, more dead than alive. They were brought to Winchcombe together in a cart. When sufficiently recovered, David (Johns) *was sentenced to seven years overseas. He returned home in the year 1878, when the writer had a long talk with him. The spot where the fight took place is kept open until this day, a hole in the side of the path leading to Farmcote."*

SUBSCRIPTION TO REWARD

JOHN BANNING,

THE "WINCHCOMB POLICEMAN."

The following Gentlemen have kindly consented to act as a

Committee of Management.

EDWARD HOLLAND, Esq., *Dumbleton Hall*
WILLIAM GIST, Esq., *Dixton Manor House*
WILLIAM DENT, Esq., *Sudeley Castle*
THE REV. EDWARD FRANCIS WITTS, *Wood Stanway*
THE REV. JOHN R. HARVEY, *Vicarage, Winchcomb*
EDMUND T. BROWNE, Esq., *High Bailiff of Winchcomb*

Treasurer.

MR. WM. TOWNSHEND, (Agent for the Gloucestershire Banking Company,) *Winchcomb*

Honorary Secretary.

MR. DENNIS TRENFIELD, Solicitor, *Winchcomb*

The gallant Conduct of Banning in apprehending David Johns, the Sweep, in the night of the 20th of February last, near Hailes Wood, (after a most desperate conflict, during which the Sweep attempted to murder him, first with a bludgeon loaded with bullets, and afterwards with a case knife, with which he severely wounded Banning on the throat and across the back of his right hand, but being at length overpowered by the undaunted courage of the Policeman, he was brought to Justice. and at the last Gloucester Assizes convicted and transported for life), comes thus forcibly recommended to the Public by the Presiding Judge of Assize, who, after passing sentence on the Prisoner, thus addressed Banning—

"Your conduct has been commended by the Grand Jury, and must be by every body who has heard it. You have shown yourself a very gallant officer. When I am giving away other people's money, I don't like to be too liberal; but under all the circumstances, I feel warranted in awarding you twenty pounds. I hope the reward I give you will not be all that you will receive."

Banning being by trade a Tailor, and the wound across his right hand having (besides lessening its strength) permanently deprived him of the use of his fore-finger, he is thus prevented from resuming his Trade, should he at any time leave the Police Force.

The Sum raised by this Subscription is therefore proposed to be laid out for his benefit in the purchase of such an Annuity as the proceeds will provide.

FORGERY and FRAUD

Two of the 'pillars of the community' on the committee appointed to manage the subscription to reward John Banning were involved in a scandal not long afterwards.

Dennis Trenfield

Dennis Trenfield was a highly respected solicitor. However, in September 1853, Robert Timbrill asked Trenfield for a loan to cover debts incurred at Cambridge University. In order to meet this request, Trenfield borrowed money from John Edwards, a farmer of Toddington. He was unable to offer security for this loan, so he gave Mr. Edwards a bond for the borrowed sum, signed by Robert Timbrill and the Reverend Edward Dupré, vicar of Temple Guiting. He had forged both signatures.

When this forgery came to light in 1858, Trenfield fled to London before the date of his trial. He attempted to commit suicide by shooting himself, sustaining serious head wounds. P.C. Smith, who escorted him back from London, testified at Trenfield's trial that his jaw was severely broken. His counsel attempted to defend his forgery by saying that he was on such intimate terms with both parties that putting their names to the bond was justifiable. The judge did not accept this defence and in five minutes the jury returned a guilty verdict. He was sentenced to ten years' penal servitude and transported. He did return to England, though probably not to Winchcombe.

Reverend John Ridout Harvey

Caught up in this scandal was Reverend Harvey, who had signed promissory notes for Mr Edwards and Mr Slatter while insolvent. According to the ***Cheltenham Chronicle***, when he signed the notes all his goods had already been seized in May 1855, and he had *"made an assignment of his living (except a* *small allowance of £100 a year to support himself, his wife and seven children) for the general benefit of his creditors."*Mr Smallridge, defending, urged that the case was *"an exceptional one, the insolvent being a clergyman having little or no knowledge of mercantile or trade transactions, and being upon most intimate terms with Mr Trenfield."* He added that the fact that the insolvent's *"goods had been sold and that he had been in needy circumstances had become notorious"*, and the lenders must have known this when they took the notes, *"the proceeds of which were intended for Trenfield's benefit"*. Harvey thought that a previous debt had been paid and that the ones he was signing would be paid. He had been *"the victim of a designing man"*.

He was sentenced to nine months' imprisonment, after which he resumed his post as Vicar at St Peter's Church. He served for another twelve years, and he was very highly regarded.

Interior of St Peter's Church, 1909

MURDER

Richard Smith, December 1865

In a very tragic case, Richard Smith, 50, retired surgeon, was charged with the murder of his wife at their house in North Street, on the corner with Chandos Street. He had killed her with a shotgun, but he was found not guilty of murder, being *non compos mentis* at the time, and committed to the Asylum at Gloucester. Apparently, several members of the family (two of his uncles, one brother and a sister) had already been committed to lunatic asylums.

At the trial, the jury were told that he and his wife had been happily married for 28 years. They were a most affectionate couple; Richard Smith was mild, gentle and usually placid. He had suffered from an almost fatal brain fever for about a month in 1846, but he continued to work as a surgeon until 1851, when one of his sons died. This made him very distressed and unable to practise.

In 1852, he was taken to see a specialist, Dr Thomas Shapter of Exeter. The doctor decided that he was suffering from *'chronic insanity'* and was liable to attacks of *'acute insanity'*. From being a professional man with a respected position as a surgeon, Richard Smith became financially dependent on his brother, living in a modest house, next to a wheelwright.

The couple lived alone in North Street, while their children lived with relatives. The youngest son, Cornelius, 15, lived with his unmarried aunt, Ann, in Gloucester House (now Cotswold House), while Martha, James, 17, and William, 20, lived with their uncle, Mr William Smith of The Farm. They did not live away from their parents through any disagreement; on the contrary it was a very close and affectionate family.

The house on the corner of North Street and Chandos Street

Evidence that the Balance of his Mind was Disturbed - Richard Smith, however, had been growing increasingly eccentric since 1851. These are some of the reports of his strange behaviour which were reported at the trial. Many witnesses said that he was convinced that his sons were in danger of being kidnapped by the police and sent to fight in the American Civil War. He would walk on tiptoe, whisper and point at the window, as if he could see someone spying on the house. There was an empty building at the back of the house, and he had the shutters and curtains closed because he thought there was a camera hidden in the building to take photographs.

Outside the house in North Street, a horse fair used to be held twice a year. One time, he came out of his house with no hat or shoes on, jumped on a pony and galloped off. Another time he negotiated the purchase of a horse and then told the dealer that, if he did not take the horse away, he would stick a skewer through it. Once, apparently, he advised a gentleman to take his horse to a public house and give it brandy and water.

He would often walk about Winchcombe without his hat and necktie, a standard of dress which was, at that time, most unconventional in a professional man. He would stop strangers and shake hands with them, while walking straight past friends and members of his family, as if he did not know them. Sergeant George Cooks testified that he once met Mr Smith sitting on the *'roadside edging'*, and another time he had asked Sergeant Cooks to sing. Several people reported seeing the former surgeon fishing with rod, line and float in the ruts of the turnpike road and the furrows of a ploughed field.

All the witnesses said that he was a kind, gentle man, although despondent at times. He was rarely violent and reports of his aggression were inexplicably against his siblings, who were always kind to him. Apparently, he once tried to turn his brother out of his house and had assaulted his nephew. He also committed random attacks against his sister's house, breaking panes of glass and throwing an umbrella through a bedroom window.

The Day of the Murder - On 27th December, 1865, Mr Smith's sons had visited their parents and held a shooting match in the fields, going after rabbits. Two loaded shotguns were left in the kitchen. The sons left the house at about 8.30 p.m. and testified that their parents were healthy and happy when they left; there was no ill-feeling at all. At about nine o'clock, the neighbour, Mary Greenhart (wife of Elisha Greenhart, the wheelwright), heard a gun apparently fired in the parlour of the house next door. The two houses had once been one and the partition was very thin, so she would have heard any argument or raised voices. She heard only chairs being moved and Mr Smith's voice. She went out into the street and walked to the corner, but returned to her own house when the Chandos Street door of the Smiths' house opened.

At eight o'clock next morning, Mrs Mary Ann Warton testified that she *'knocked at the brewhouse door'* for milk, as she did every day. She knew the family well as she had lived with them for two years as a servant nineteen years before. Unusually, Mr Smith answered the door, and he seemed to stammer, not answering her enquiry about his wife.

At nine o'clock, Mr Smith went to his brother's house and told his sons that their mother had been shot. He gave James the key to the house in North Street, and then he went to his sister's house to tell Cornelius. He told his son that the gun had been in his hand, and it had gone off, shooting the poor boy's mother. Mr Smith then started to walk to Cheltenham. P.C. Hinder went after him and caught him up at Southam. It appears that he had no intention of running away, but planned to return.

To his great distress, James, accompanied by Joseph Payne, one of William Smith's employees, found his mother lying on the parlour floor with a wound in her neck which Thomas Newman, surgeon, said would have killed her instantly. The husband had been alone all night with the wife he had tragically killed. His sons asked the police to keep close watch on him, as they feared he might commit suicide.

Richard Smith was tried at the Spring Assizes in Gloucester on April Fool's Day, 1865. In their extensive newspaper report, ***The Gloucestershire Chronicle*** observed that, as the jury left the courtroom, the defendant's *"eyes were of a leaden hue, but they spoke of latent madness."* He was found not guilty of murder, on the grounds of insanity. He was kept in Gloucester Gaol for a year and then sent to Broadmoor Lunatic Asylum, where he remained until his death in 1883. None of his children inherited the genetic tendency towards madness.

MURDER and SUICIDE

Thomas Wallins, 1904

In June 1904, Thomas Wallins (25), a worker on the new Cheltenham-Honeybourne railway at Greet, left his lodgings in Hailes Street as usual at 6:00 am. However, instead of going to work, he bought cigarettes and a pint of ale at the Plasterers' Arms, which always opened early in the morning. An hour later he returned and cut the throat of his landlord's daughter, Mrs Louisa Bingham (23), a young woman with whom it appears that he was infatuated. It seems likely that he killed her in a fit of jealous rage because he saw a love letter she had written to his brother.

With her life blood draining away, Louisa Bingham fled out of the garden into the alley and re-entered the house by the side door, falling into the arms of her father, Samuel Robins. Wallins then slashed his own throat before staggering after her, only to find the door barred against him. He struggled up the alley to Hailes Street, leaving a copious trail of blood, and entered the house through the front door. Doctor Cox was called, but, by the time he arrived, both the murderer and his victim were dead.

Until two years before, Louisa had lived with her husband, George Bingham, a fruit salesman, of 118 Holly Place, Duddeston Mill Road in Birmingham. The marriage did not last long, although they parted on amicable terms. When she left her husband, Louisa got a job in a lamp factory in Birmingham and moved in with Joseph Wallins, who was living at the same lodging house as his brother, Thomas. Louisa's parents had moved to Winchcombe, where Mr Robins was given a position as a messenger at the Isolation Hospital in Langley Road. Three months before the tragedy, they suggested she come to live with them.

The steam navvy, working on the Cheltenham-Honeybourne railway line

Navvies cutting out under Greet Bridge where the steam navvy cannot penetrate
Photograph reproduced with the kind permission of Tim Petchey

Thomas Wallins, formerly a carter working for a brewery firm in Birmingham, had accompanied Louisa Bingham to Winchcombe in order to look for a new job. He had helped her with her luggage, but all the witnesses at the inquest testified that they were not in a relationship. He took lodgings with her parents who kept a boarding house in Hailes Street for railway employees. Apparently, Wallins' behaviour had been normal the previous evening, except that he took a razor belonging to Mr Robins out of a drawer and sharpened it on a strop, saying that he was going to shave off his moustache. He did not shave it off. At that time, Louisa was bottling ginger beer to sell to the workers building the railway. On the morning of the murder, the landlord at the Plasterers' Arms reported that Wallins appeared calm and collected. He asked for a piece of paper, on which he wrote in pencil, shielding the writing with his hand. This piece of paper was never found.

The front of the Robins's house showing entrance to alley

On his return, he went into the room where Louisa Bingham was writing letters, removed his boots and placed them under the bench near her chair. For some reason now unknown, she suddenly jumped up from her seat and rushed outside. Mrs Sarah Nash, a neighbour, heard a scream, looked over and saw Louisa lying full length on the garden path. Wallins was standing over her with an open razor in his hand. Mrs Nash testified that, *"Despite the prostrate woman's entreaties and struggles, he slashed her across the face with the razor and then deliberately cut her throat."* She shouted at the attacker, and this distracted him so that his poor victim was able to get away and struggle into the house.

This photograph is of the back of the Robins's house. Sarah Nash, the neighbour, is standing by the door, where the murder was committed. Mrs Robins is on the right, standing next to a policeman. The dark patch in front of the doorway is a pool of blood. The table close by is that over which Wallins was bending when he cut his own throat.

Louisa's distraught mother looked out of the door and shouted at Wallins; then she saw him draw the razor across his own throat. He ran after Mrs Robins, but she knocked him off the doorstep and slammed the door in his face. He then stumbled into the street and entered through the front door, the open razor still in his hand. He lurched across the floor and would doubtless have attacked Mr Robins if Frank Sales, another lodger, had not knocked him down and wrested the razor from him, before running for the doctor. Samuel Robins, who was cradling his daughter's head, spent twenty minutes listening to the groans of the murderer before Thomas Wallins finally died. Witnesses testified that Thomas Wallins was habitually reserved and morose, and he was *"standoffish"* to Louisa Bingham, although he followed her everywhere. She objected to this and kept on telling him, in no uncertain terms, not to follow her, but he would not be deterred.

The Robins' house in the centre, with the bedroom windows open

'Waiting to start.' Undertaker's men with the coffin of Louisa Bingham outside the house. The alley is on the left.

The funeral procession passing Winchcombe Police Station

Louisa Bingham left three letters. One was to her husband; one was to a girl friend, and the following one was to Joseph Wallins, brother of her murderer, who had remained in Birmingham:

"Dear Joe – I take the pleasure of writing you a few lines, hoping you are quite well, as it leaves me. Dearest, I was glad to hear that you are happy. I know the people you are with will do you good, and that Louie will look after you and see you don't have too much beer. You must not think of coming here yet as there are no lodgings to be had. I will promise you, my darling, to come and see you soon. Don't make me feel unhappy because I have gone through enough as it is with one thing and another. Dear Joe, I send you the right measurement of my finger and I hope you will send me one. When I come to see you, I shall come a better woman than I have been. I shall come nice. I hope you will be true to the one that loves you so well, my own darling husband, as I hope you soon will be anyhow. From your own little Looloo. Xxxx"

Mourners at the graveside after the service

The inquest returned a verdict of **Wilful Murder** and ***Felo-de-se***, a Latin term for 'Felon of himself'. Even at the beginning of the Twentieth Century, almost all victims of suicide were assumed to be ***non compos mentis*** at the time of the killing, but the jury were convinced that Wallins was perfectly sane and had committed wilful murder on himself as well as his victim.

Burials of such felons used to take place between 9:00 p.m. and midnight, with no rites, no mourners or clergy present, and the location would be kept secret by the authorities. However, the Coroner reported that Wallins *"had a right to be buried in the parish churchyard with such decent formalities and ceremonies as may be required and as are usual.... All the barbarous customs such as burying a man under the crossroads and driving a stake through him were abolished by the Internments Act of 1882."*

Spectators at Louisa Bingham's funeral standing on Cemetery path

Frederick Fawdry, May 17th, 1917

In 1853, Alfred Reeks opened his butcher's shop at 23 High Street, Winchcombe. Sixty four years later, on April 20th 1917, he died. Although he had ten children, he left the shop to his nephew, Frederick Fawdry, who had joined him in the business and lived at the shop with the housekeeper, Rose Page. Fawdry was 39 years old when Alfred Reeks died, and he had been engaged for thirteen years to Eliza Emma Mathews, niece of Edward Day who ran the Town Flour Mill. We can only speculate why he was engaged to be married for such a long time but reluctant to solemnise the union. Fawdry had apparently had a long history of depression and anxiety.

Eliza Mathews, the murder victim. Photograph reproduced with the kind permission of Tina Bennett

Early in 1917, Edward Adlard, magistrate, who knew Fawdry, arranged for him to go on holiday to recover from stress. On Easter Tuesday, when he returned, Dr. Cox, who had known him all his life, thought him no better.

On April 6th, when friends brought Fawdry to Dr Cox's surgery insisting they could no longer look after him, he was certified 'a person of unsound mind', suitable for admission to an asylum. Miss Mathews, however, still wanted to marry him, convinced that her care and devotion would restore him to perfect health.

When Mr Reeks died, the banns had, at last, been called and the wedding set for April. Fawdry cancelled the wedding, indicating that he was deeply upset about his uncle's death. An engagement was a serious matter, and Fawdry was legally bound to pay Eliza for breach of promise. Suddenly, he changed his mind and decided on a very hasty ceremony. Accordingly, Eliza went to St Peter's Church at 8:00 a.m. on May 15th. She was left waiting at the altar. Disturbed at the delay, the vicar sent for the bridegroom, who turned up in his bloody butcher's smock and paced around the churchyard. Eventually, he was persuaded to remove the smock and enter the church.

Frederick Fawdry

After the ceremony, they walked back to the shop, had lunch and later tea with Rose Page who had stayed on as housekeeper after the death of Alfred Reeks. After tea, Eliza asked Frederick to fetch her some night clothes from her uncle's house, but he refused, saying he was tired.

Reeks' butcher's shop in the High Street, now a florist's

At the inquest, Rose Page testified that she collected Eliza's clothes, but, on her return, found that the bride had fallen asleep. Fawdry then said he was going out for a drink. He actually went to the home of Ernest Smith Wood, the solicitor, who sent him away, arranging to see him in the morning. About midnight he returned, but Rose said that he was restless. Next morning, Fawdry started work in the shop and at 6 o'clock, together with Alfred Reeks' brother, George, slaughtered a bullock, preparing the meat with a boning knife. At 8 o'clock, the newly-weds had breakfast with Rose Page. The latter went into the kitchen, and, a few minutes later, she heard a scream. She rushed back into the dining room just in time to see Fawdry cutting his own throat. She called for help; George Reeks and a porter, George Cutting, ran in from the alley alongside the shop, but it was too late, Frederick and Eliza were both dead.

At the inquest, Dr. Cox and the other witnesses testified that Eliza Fawdry was found lying with her head on a small table and her feet on a fender. The chair on which she was sitting had fallen over. Her hair was pulled back from her face and, at the back of her head, her hair was pulled down. Her throat had been cut with a single blow, and there was no sign of a struggle. The murderer was lying against the wall, dying. The boning knife was nearby. Many people attended Eliza's funeral, which was held on the following Saturday. Her body was arrayed in her wedding dress, and her coffin was carried by her brother, her brother-in-law and two cousins to St Peter's Church, where it was left overnight. She was buried in the grave of her grandparents, Mr and Mrs Day.

DOUBLE TRAGEDY AT WINCHCOMBE
"The butcher's shop and residence where Mr Fred Fawdry murdered his bride and afterwards committed suicide the morning after his marriage, on Wednesday, May 16th. It was snapped on the morning of the tragedy, and children can be seen looking at the house with awed curiosity."
Cheltenham Chronicle and Gloucestershire Graphic, May 1917

"SAD DEATH OF A WINCHCOMBE TRADESMAN: A VERDICT OF SUICIDE"

The Cheltenham Chronicle and Gloucestershire Graphic told this tragic story in March 1913. Mr Thomas Martin (42), cycle dealer and repairer by ***The George Inn*** in Winchcombe, killed himself while the balance of his mind was disturbed. Thomas Martin had been suffering from influenza for a week, but, in spite of the care of Dr. G. Ralph Cox and his wife, his condition deteriorated, and he developed measles, having a temperature of 105° and suffering from delirium. Dr Cox warned Annie Martin not to leave him alone, but, after she gave him some custard on Tuesday 4th March, she left him for a few minutes, finding the bedroom door locked on her return.

She ran for Albert Day, licensee of The George Hotel, and he and his son burst open the door to find the invalid on the floor with blood all around and wounds to his neck. When the doctor came at 1:45 pm, he dressed the wounds and hoped Martin would recover. However, on his return, the injured man's breathing was considerably worse and he died soon after.

Cause of death was recorded as *'bronchial pneumonia, accelerated by loss of blood and haemorrhage'*. When P.C. John Hughes arrived, he found a blood-stained pen-knife under the night-commode which was three-quarters full of blood. Mr Martin left two letters. The first read *"I am bound to do this mad act, as I cannot live. Something has burst in my inside."* The second: *"I pray you will all forgive me doing this mad act. It is impossible to live with this burst in my inside."* Dr. Cox said that nothing had burst inside him; his fear was just a delusion.

Thomas Martin's cycle shop is on the right of this picture
Photograph reproduced with the kind permission of Tim Petchey

SUICIDE

In ***The Winchcombe and Sudeley Record,*** November 1891, Emma Dent writes about the old custom of burying someone who committed suicide outside consecrated ground, at a crossroads. She told the story of Dab, who committed suicide and was buried at the crossroads near Alderton. A stake was plunged through his body to keep him quiet, and it took root, becoming known locally as 'Dab's Elm'.

"THE BLACK WIDOW"

Gordon and Ann Parsons told the following story in the ***Millenium Book: Winchcombe: Our Home - Our Heritage.*** It concerns the sister of an old woman called Agatha Pollard who used to live in Silk Mill Lane, by the gasworks.

They write that Agatha *"... would undoubtedly have been thought a witch had she lived in medieval Winchcombe. This is not to say that there was anything sinister about Agatha Pollard – Gatha to all the locals – but the fact that she lived surrounded by cats ... and her severe speech impediment, the result we understand of an hereditary condition leading early in life to profound deafness, would certainly have aroused dangerous suspicions in past ages."*

......

"As my wife and I checked out our shared, partial understanding of Gatha's tortuous tales, one developing story started to amaze us. Gatha had an elder sister who had apparently been left well off when her husband died. She had then acquired a much younger 'admirer'. Gatha naturally had no time for this 'gold-digger'. When he finally tired of waiting, her 80-year old sister was so incensed that she had gone off to Swindon to hire hit men to break his legs ... so that he would never dance with another woman!"

"Daily communiqués from Gatha began to make us believe she had lost all touch with reality. Apparently, the hit men had taken her sister's money but reneged on their commitment, so she had returned to Swindon to confront them, under the Trades' Descriptions Act presumably! They then did their duty and beat up the would-be Lothario-cum-Fred Astaire. It was all one great comic fantasy, surely?

Oh no! The headlines hit the tabloids making the 'Black Widow' a reality. The judge at Winchester Assizes sent the hit men to jail, but what was he to do with this 80 year old Medea with terminal cancer? He put her on two years' probation, during which time she did the decent thing!"

Some of Winchcombe's special constables (1920)
John Oakey is seated in the centre

JOHN OAKEY'S REMINISCENCES OF CRIMES

John Oakey was a local builder, born in 1847. In 1936-7, he wrote a book of his memories of life in Winchcombe:

(pp. 75-6) 'There was plenty of crime locally in my young days, lamb and poultry stealing, wheat, bacon, grocery and the like, while a great deal of poaching was also carried on. It was not unusual to see constables searching for loot stuff, nearly always at the same houses. It seemed there was no need for warrants or any authority for searching in those days.

One case I particularly remember was that of three men stealing bacon hams from over the oven at Mr. Sam Willis' bakery at the bottom of the Castle Pitch. It was usual for people with no conveniences to dry their bacon and hams over these ovens. The loader for Mr. Willis was persuaded by two other men to let them have a key, and he was to share the booty. They took about twenty hams and hid them in a big stone gout near Tythe Court, till the searching was over, knowing that both their cottages would be searched. They obtained the hams later, but, when the loader went for his share, they repudiated him and he never got a rasher. The robbery caused a great stir at the time. One of the men, R.W., admitted the whole thing when working for me in 1880, when he was then a very old man.

Night poaching for pheasants was common. Two keepers I knew were shot by poachers. One whose name was Pidgeon lost an arm. He was for many years lodge keeper at Southam. Another, John Last, was shot through the arm but just managed to save amputation. A poacher from Broadway shot him and served imprisonment. Game was more rigidly preserved then than now.'

'George Hicks was a great poacher (nothing worse). He went to Gloucester Jail for these offences over forty times, and he used to boast that he went so often that he kept his cell aired. He never gave police or game keepers the slightest trouble, he was so polite. On one occasion Squire Dent met him in the street: "George," he says, "I understand you had as many as eighty brace of fish from my pond last night." "To be exact, sir," George replies, "it was eighty-two brace."'(p. 86)

'The first constable I remember was named Coleman. One morning, early, he met a well known character carrying two buckets on a yoke at the bottom of the Back Lane. The constable caught him up and the man began making excuses about having to carry water for washing. The constable dipped his finger in one bucket and on tasting it found it was port wine, just stolen from the Abbey.

Another who seemed to have a mania for stealing fowls, was told on his last conviction, that if he was caught again it would mean transportation. After being met by a constable coming from Stoney Cockbury with a bag of fowls, he threw the bag down and ran away across the fields. The constable, knowing him, did not follow, but took charge of the fowls. In the morning a cowman (Isaac James) at Rushbury Farm, Cockbury, just opposite, found the man hanging in the cow stalls, dead.

Up to the year 1840, body-snatching was frequent. An aunt told me that she had seen two bodies in a loft at the top of Duck Street which had been stolen from the churchyard. Men often watched the graves of relatives for a few nights after burial.'(pp. 76-7)

FORMER PUNISHMENTS

Ducking Stool

The Ducking Stool was a punishment designed for women accused of being scolds, of quarrelling or committing minor offences. A scold was a term given to a gossip, or a bad-tempered woman. The accused was strapped into a sturdy chair, which was fastened to a long wooden beam fixed as a seesaw on the edge of the River Isbourne in Duck Street (now Vineyard Street). The chair would then be swung over the river by the use of the free-moving arm. The woman would then be ducked into the freezing cold water.

Sometimes the woman was only immersed for just a few seconds, but, in some circumstances, this punishment process could be continuously repeated over the course of a day. This form of public torture prevailed from the early seventeenth through to the early nineteenth century.

Emma Dent, writing in ***The Annals of Winchcombe and Sudeley,*** reported that: *"The ducking-stool was another instrument of torture in Winchcombe, and which was remembered by some of the oldest inhabitants (of 1850) to have existed at the bottom of Duck Street, which, probably, thence received its name. The ducking-stool was generally established in some favourite rendezvous of a town, or where the women were in the habit of drawing water; so, when any unfortunate culprit was carried to the brook, it is not difficult to imagine the scene of commotion and excitement that followed; all Winchcombe turned out to see the poor woman dipped and the ardour of her tongue cooled. With pity we turn from the poor suffering women, and thank God that the law of the land has now abolished punishments made a hundredfold more cruel by their publicity." (p. 148)*

John Oakey built the bridge at the bottom of Duck Street, and he wrote about finding *"the remains of the old Ducking Stool, which was used for ducking refractory women, this being the reason for the name Duck Street." (p. 30)*

Whipping Post

Emma Dent noted in 1877 that, when the monasteries were dissolved, *"The immediate effect of the change was very disastrous to the poor, who, beside all the customary hospitality, and relief in want and sickness being suddenly stopped, too often found themselves thrown out of employment, by the new landlords turning the lands they used to cultivate into pasture.*

No wonder, then, that thousands were forced into vagrant habits, to check which severe laws were passed, and whipping-posts and stocks everywhere set up, and were in common use for punishing 'vagrants and sturdy beggars', both men and women, up to the end of the last (eighteenth) century.

In Winchcombe the whipping-post was still in existence A.D. 1800, when Mr. Castle, of North Street (now in his ninety-second year) recollects one in front of the Town Hall, a post fixed in the ground with iron rings, screwed in with hinges, leaving just sufficient room for the arms and legs to pass between the iron and the post; they were locked in, and then the whipping commenced.

Mr. Castle saw six women flogged there in the year 1800; they were stripped to the waist and flogged till the blood ran down their backs; their offence was 'hedge pulling'. The man who whipped them was Frank Crow; he also recollects the names of some of the women, but as their descendants are still living in Winchcombe (in 1877), *it is but right to withhold them.*

M. J. Booth.

J. Rushton.

Whipping Post and Ducking Stool, Duck Street, Winchcombe.

Sometimes the stocks were combined with the whipping-post; but gradually the punishment went out of practice, and now our Winchcombe whipping-post has altogether disappeared, the stocks alone remaining in remembrance of bygone days, and are to be seen in gloomy shadow under the present Town Hall." (p. 147)

Stocks

The Stocks were originally intended as a means of confining offenders once they had committed a crime. However, they were eventually used as a means of punishment in themselves. They were normally used for punishing petty criminals. George Greening told his son, Harold, that *"it was generally a drunken case or a quarrelling case, something like that. The more serious cases were sent to Gloucester for punishment."*

Public humiliation was a major part of the punishment, so they were a popular form of entertainment for passers by. They were placed right in the centre of town, and those being punished would be well known to passers-by. This brought down more shame on their heads.

The offenders could be confined for long periods, and they were left in the stocks in all weathers. The helpless miscreant would usually be subjected to a barrage of mockery and abuse, and pelted with any missiles which came to hand. Use your imagination to understand what vile things might have been thrown at unpopular criminals.

Winchcombe's stocks were still in use as late as 1860 when a man was put in them for the crime of drunkenness. They are very unusual in having seven holes; a fact which has given rise to a suggestion that there was a persistent one-legged offender.

The Court of Summary Justice (Petty Sessions)

In Winchcombe Museum, there is a folder entitled ***"Caught in Winchcombe"***, which lists the cases brought to the magistrates from 1877 to 1894. Most cases bear witness to the poverty in the town at that time. People were fined for 'scrumping' apples, stealing turnips from a field or collecting firewood. They were taken before the magistrate for poaching, for begging, for having too many people in their houses and for not sending their children to school.

Playing pitch and toss on the highway was a crime, as was keeping a dog without a licence and delivering bread without having scales. Drunkenness was rife because the pubs were open from 6:00 a.m. until nearly midnight. There were six Cider Mills around and most householders made their own cider or wine.

Harold Greening's memories

Penalties were severe, as we can learn from Harold Greening's account of when his grandfather, Henry, once *"got locked up for taking a bit of firewood home."*

He was working in the quarry at Farmcote Bottom *"when he got into this trouble, and he was locked up one night at The Police Station at Winchcombe (in Stancombe Lane), and when he was tried for what he was supposed to have done, he was sent to Gloucester for seven days' hard labour for bringing a stick home! He was on the tread-mill 20 minutes on and 20 minutes off. If you missed your step then you had some skinned shins, so you had to keep stepping – treading the wind it was called. He was tried at The Town Hall at Winchcombe."*

Weird Stories

Grotesques from St Peter's Church

INTRODUCTION

Many people are still superstitious, refusing to walk under ladders, throwing spilt salt over their left shoulders and taking down Christmas decorations on Twelfth Night. It is not surprising that people were even more superstitious in the past. In the ***Winchcombe and Sudeley Record,*** Emma Dent made a comprehensive record of local superstitions:

In August 1891, Emma Dent recalled that *"'Charming' for the white mouth, thrush or canker was a very common practice in Winchcombe. The oldest inhabitants can remember how children suffering from those complaints were taken to be charmed by the blacksmith, Mr Bridges, 'old Thatcher Smith's wife', and others. The incantations were mysteriously muttered over the infant, the words were sometimes taken from Scripture, when one thumb of the charmer was placed on the mystic text, and the other in the mouth of the suffering child."*

In September 1892, she described a very strange ritual to determine guilt. *"Many stories are told in Winchcombe of the old ceremony connected with the superstitious use of the Bible and Key, the directions for which run thus: They must be bound tightly together, the key being placed on the 16th verse of the 1st chapter of Ruth. The bowl of the key must then be balanced by two persons on their first fingers.*

Suppose information to be desired on a particular subject, such as 'Are your suspicions correct as to a theft?' then if, while the second person repeats the verse, the Bible turn towards you, your suspicions are well founded; if groundless, the book will remain stationary. During the performance care must be taken not to divulge the name of the person about whom information is to be sought.

This experiment was resorted to so recently as in 1832, when a case of theft was brought before the Magistrates. A Mr White had lost some property, and it was agreed to try the case by the Bible. One of the women present named the suspected person three times, while another recited the words: 'If it turn to thee, Thou art the thief, and we are free.' The key then turned on poor Mr Blucher, the suspected person, who was punished accordingly."

In September 1891, she reported that *"'Water running against the sun' is also a specific* (medicine for weak eyes), *and it has been a custom to fetch it from Langley Hill for this purpose, where the water runs from west to east. Though, on the contrary, the stream from St Kenelm's Well runs from east to west, yet universal was the fame of its healing properties."*

The Winchcombe blacksmith, Charles Gardner, told Mrs Dent that a man employed by his father would pull a wrongly placed nail out of the horse's hoof and hammer it into the wall in order to prevent the horse from going lame. As late as the 1930s, when Mr. Adlard, the owner of Postlip Mills, died, the workers filed past his body to pay their respects. Every one of them touched his hand. His daughter asked why they did this, and the foreman told her it was, *"To prevent the spirit from haunting them."*

These are a few of the local superstitions, but, with Winchcombe's ancient and colourful history, it is to be expected that there are also many stories of ghosts and hauntings, witches and wizards in and around the town. In the following pages are some of them.

BELAS KNAP

Belas Knap, the Neolithic long barrow found two miles south of Winchcombe, is well known to be 'a place of power'. When it was excavated, the remains of at least 37 human skeletons from the Neolithic period were discovered. Some say that Belas comes from the Old English word 'bel' for a beacon, others that it derives from an ancient storm god Baal ('Belus' in Latin); however all agree that Knap is Old English for a hill top.

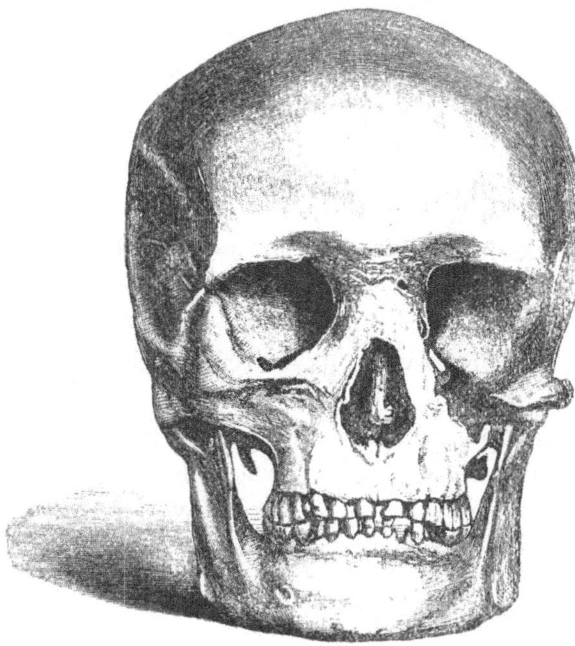

SKULL found in Belas Knap Barrow.

Various supernatural experiences

People have reported various kinds of supernatural experiences. Interestingly, it is ghosts of monks, not Stone Age men, that people have claimed to see here. Some people say that they can see the ley lines. Apparently, there is a sixteen mile ley line from Pershore to Winchcombe, which then converges with other ley lines. Visitors have also claimed to see greenish orbs, or to sense a 'presence', sometimes feeling a 'pins-and-needles' sensation and a chill; sometimes hearing slow, rhythmic drums that do not fade but stop suddenly.

A Hedge Druid's Blog

In 2013, Gwas Myrddyn, a Hedge Druid, wrote in his blog that, at Belas Knap, he was shown an unusual energy formation. The energy flowed the full length of the top of the structure, and he recognised the image as a snake with its jaws around the world. There are stories in other mythologies of the giant serpent devouring its own tail and encircling the world.

Gwas Myrddyn tells that he stood in the 'forked tail' feature at the back of the mound, and noticed that others had left straw offerings and sticks here too, so he realised that Belas Knap is an active site for modern pagans. He deduced that the purpose of the 'snake eating the world' was to destroy outside energies, thus protecting and preserving the energies of the buried spirits.

It is interesting to note that, when Belas Knap was excavated in 1863, Frederick Simmons found a curious-looking flint, about 5 inches long, serrated on one edge. He showed it to Dr. Bird, an antiquarian, who saw this as proof that it was a Druidical tomb.

A Scary Experience!

Bob Meredith reports that, near the end of the Twentieth Century, a family from the Midlands, visiting Belas Knap on a warm day without any wind, chose to have their lunch on top of the mound to enjoy the beautiful view. They spread out their picnic, but suddenly the tablecloth *"leapt"* into the air sending their meal flying in all directions.

WINCHCOMBE ABBEY

King Offa established a convent of nuns at Winchcombe in 787 A.D. and his successor, King Kenulf, added a monastery of monks in 798 A.D., when the foundation became a double monastery and the building of the Abbey started. The royal foundation provided for a community of 300 monks. The Abbey provided work for lots of servants, as well as craftsmen and labourers to work on the buildings. Pilgrims to St Kenelm's shrine and to Hailes Abbey had brought revenue for the town. However, the Abbey was dissolved by Henry VIII in 1539, and now there is nothing left of the Abbey buildings. Some people think one of the monks must have laid a curse on those who profited from the dissolution: Thomas Cromwell, Henry's Vicar-General and primarily responsible for the dissolution of Winchcombe Abbey, was beheaded in 1540, exactly one year after the Abbey surrendered. The Abbey and manor of Winchcombe were granted to Thomas Seymour in 1547; he had all the stone taken to Sudeley to rebuild the castle, but his wife died in 1548, and he was executed in 1549.

It seems that some of the monks never left Winchcombe. People have claimed to hear plainchant and other religious songs being chanted at midnight in the vicinity of the Abbey grounds. The ghosts of monks are often seen around the town, usually near the site of the old Abbey, especially in Cowl Lane and Abbey Terrace. However, there are also reports of sightings in the Pyke Bank area (now known as Bicks Lane) and on the roads around Winchcombe, notably Castle Street and near the Tithe Barn at Postlip Hall which was probably a Twelfth Century Chapel.

They are usually in black habits, although there are reports that they have been seen wearing grey or white, and they have their hoods over their heads. Sometimes they have no feet and seem to be gliding along a path a couple of feet below the road, where the road level used to be five hundred years ago. Strangely, an apparition that has been seen at the Railway Station seems to glide two feet above the ground!

In May, 1892, Mrs Dent recorded a piece of Winchcombe's history which concerned the Abbey Church: "*Evil spirits were associated with the smell of sulphur; when candles burnt blue they were supposed to be present, and sulphur was burnt to disperse them.*" William of Malmesbury "*chronicled that Winchcombe Church in 1091 was struck by lightning, when a thunderbolt fell with such force that it greatly damaged the tower, threw down a crucifix, and an image of St Mary. A thick smoke with a suffocating, sulphurous smell then burst forth and filled the Church, till the Monks went round with holy water, incense, and the relics of the saints, chanting psalms.*"

Rebus for Whitefriars stained glass, found in the bottom right hand corner of the stained glass window on the west wall, NW corner, of St Peter's Church.

SUDELEY CASTLE

"Old Nick went out upon a prowl,
An' cumed to Winchcombe, thuck dark 'ole,
But 'a got stuck fast in Sudeley Lane,
So swore as 'e'd never cum thur agyain."
(Verse printed in Emma Dent's ***Annals of Winchcombe and Sudeley)***

Sudeley Castle has had a dramatic history since it was built in the twelfth century. Not surprisingly, there are lots of reports of ghosts and unexplained happenings. Here are a few stories:

Catherine Parr

Queen Catherine Parr was Henry VIII's sixth wife, and, when he died, she married Thomas Seymour, First Baron Seymour of Sudeley. Sadly, she died six days after the birth of her daughter, Mary, but her troubles did not end there.

When the castle was 'slighted' by the parliamentarians during the Civil War, to prevent its use as a military fortification, the chapel in which she had been buried was a ruin. In her ***Annals,*** (pp 315-7) Emma Dent reported on the opening of her tomb in 1782, quoting an account by Mr Brookes of Reading, who was present. The former Queen's leaden coffin was discovered and opened by John Lucas, a local farmer. He ripped up the top of the coffin and found her body wrapped in several layers of linen. *"His unwarrantable curiosity led him also to make an incision through the seer cloths which covered on of the arms of the corpse, the flesh of which, at that time, was white and moist."*

A year later, Mr Brookes dug up the coffin again, but *"the body was then grown quite fetid, and the flesh where the incision had been made was brown and in a state of putrefaction, in consequence of the air having been let in upon it."*

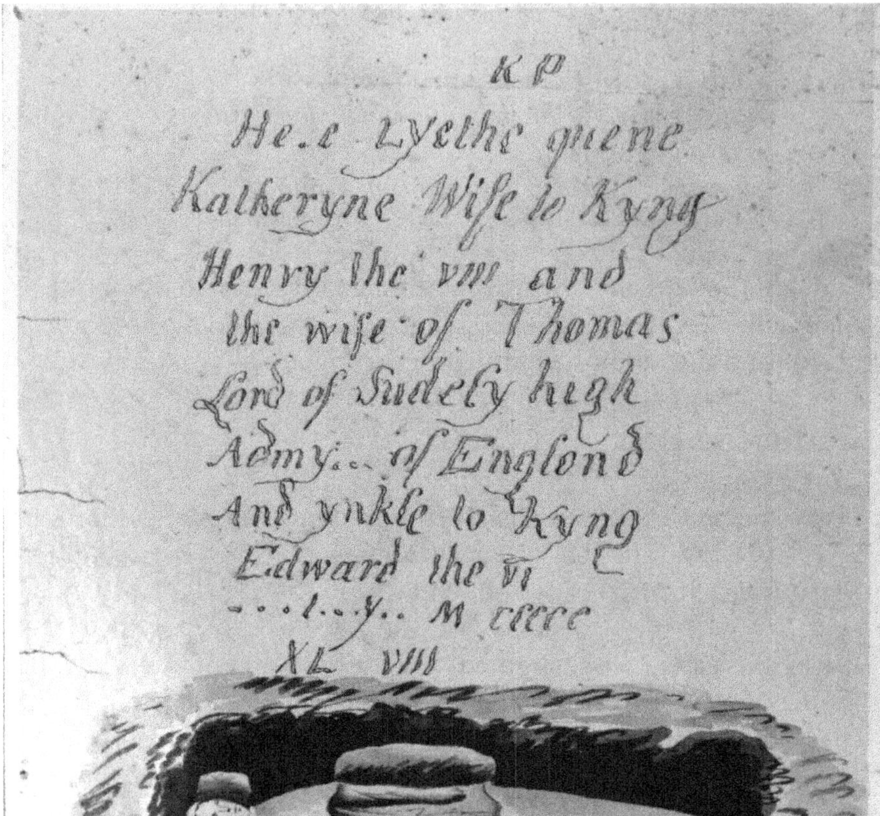

RUBBING FROM QUEEN KATHERINE PARR'S COFFIN

Mr. E.T. Browne took the rubbing on the blue paper, as he states in a letter (1817), quoted in Mrs. Dent's "Annals of Winchcombe and Sudeley", at the time he, and the then Vicar of Winchcombe, Mr. Lates, reburied the desecrated remains of Katherine Parr in the Chandos vault.

Mrs Dent reports that the coffin was opened again in 1784, 1786 and 1792. On this last occasion, *"the tomb was violated; the tenant then occupying the Castle, in the most incredible manner allowing a party of inebriated men to dig a fresh grave for the coffin. The details of their work are too dreadful to give or dwell upon, but the tradition lingers in Winchcombe that each one of that Bacchanalian band met with an untimely and horrible end."* Apparently they handled it very roughly and re-buried it upside down. Mrs Dent gives no details of their horrible ends, but John Lucas told the local doctor, John Phythian, that the Queen's ghost had appeared to him one night as he walked past her grave, and he went mad.

Frederick Simmons writes that, one day, Emma Dent asked him to mend a blind in her bedroom. After completing the task, he had to walk through the Chandos Room. It was evening and, *"to my annoyance, my candle went suddenly out!! In a most extraordinary manner, but I took little notice of it, as I could find my way around the place without a light. Having got nearly through the room, a lady passed me (on my right hand side). I distinctly heard the rustle of her silk dress and also felt the draught of air caused by the rapidity of her walking. Of course, I thought it was Mrs Dent and felt gratified that I had done the blind just in time."*

When he got downstairs, he found that Mrs Dent had been in the library all the time. He then adds *"some time back, I had taken a tooth from Catherine Parr's coffin, (when her remains were taken from the 'Chandos Vault' to be put in the new sarcophagus in Sudeley Castle Chapel), and in this same Chandos Room there was another tooth which was presented to Mrs Dent by E. T. Browne Esq., High Bailiff of Winchcombe, in 1828, and he got possession of it at the time her grave in the Chapel was so*

ruthlessly treated by Bacchanalians, at the Castle Hotel. !!! Could it be so! – that the ghost of 'Kateryn' was permitted to roam over those old precincts – 'making night hideous' – and to fill with awe those who had been guilty of robbing the dead! ..."
Not surprisingly, he returned the tooth to the coffin!

There are more recent reports that the Queen's restless spirit haunts the castle. A lady in a flowing green dress in Tudor style has been seen near the nursery, looking out of windows and walking through the gardens. At times, the sightings are linked with a child's desperate sobs and an apple-scented fragrance.

A contemporary woodcut of Prince Rupert and Boye

Boye, Prince Rupert's Hunting Poodle

A woodcut from the English Civil War showing a shaggy-maned poodle, like Boye, confronting a short-haired Roundhead dog.

During the Civil War, Sudeley was the headquarters of Prince Rupert, nephew to King Charles I, and the castle is thought to be haunted by Boye, his favourite hunting dog. Rupert was a valiant soldier and a very capable military commander. He epitomised the 'dashing cavalier', and Boye went everywhere with his master, fighting equally fiercely in the Royalist cause.

In an age where everyone believed in witchcraft, it was easy for the Parliamentarians to portray the Royalist cause as Satanic, the handsome and successful Rupert of being in league with the Devil, and Boye of being his familiar. In response, Royalist satirists mocked these accusations by publishing exaggerated claims to portray the Roundheads as gullible fools, suggesting that Boye was the Devil in disguise, Prince Rupert's shape-shifting familiar, or a 'Lapland Lady' transformed into a giant white dog. Boye was portrayed as invulnerable to attack, able to find hidden treasure and to catch bullets fired at Rupert.

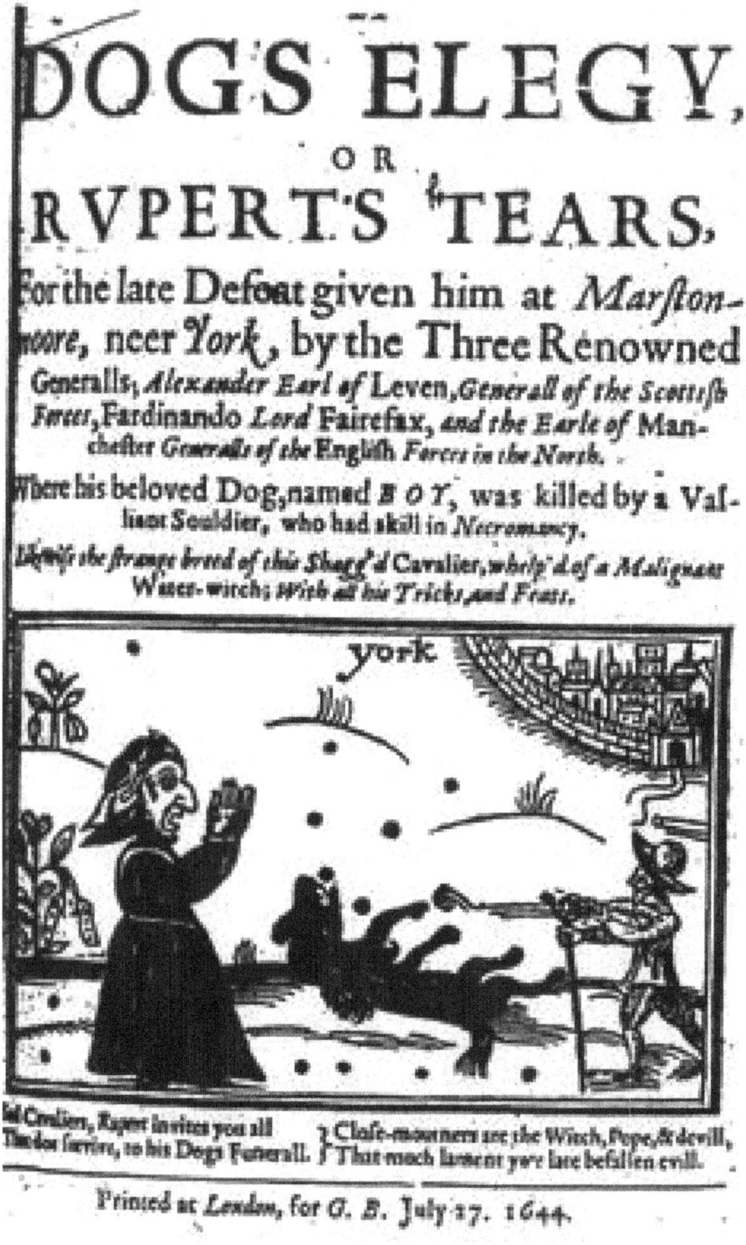
DOGS ELEGY,

OR

RVPERTS TEARS,

For the late Defeat given him at *Marston-moore*, neer *York*, by the Three Renowned Generalls, *Alexander Earl of* Leven, *Generall of the Scottish Forces*, Fardinando *Lord* Fairefax, *and the Earle of* Manchester *Generalls of the* English *Forces in the North.*

Where his beloved Dog, named *BOY*, was killed by a Valliant Souldier, who had skill in *Necromancy.*

Likewise the strange breed of this Shagg'd Cavalier, *whelp'd of a Malignant* Water-witch; *With all his Tricks, and Feats.*

Sad Cavaliers, Rupert invites you all
That doe survive, to his Dogs Funerall.
Close-mourners are the Witch, Pope, & devill,
That much lament yo'r late befallen evill.

Printed at *London*, for *G. B.* July 17. 1644.

A pamphlet reporting Boye's death at the hands of a soldier skilled in necromancy.

The Royalists promoted Boye, their adopted mascot, to the rank of Sergeant-Major-General. He died heroically during the Battle of Marston Moor in 1644. He had been left safely tied up in the Royalist camp, but he escaped and chased after Rupert. The battle went badly for the Royalists, and Rupert was forced to flee the field. Boye was killed during the ensuing fighting, while in the act of pulling a roundhead from his horse. His spirit is now said to haunt Sudeley Castle, as people report feeling him breathing on their legs or pushing against them from behind.

Janet

Sudeley Castle is also supposedly haunted by a formidable housekeeper from Scotland, known as 'Janet', who retired in the early 1950s and lived in a cottage in Rushley Lane. Apparently, she often sat at the top of the servants' stairs to stop the men from visiting the female staff at night. She appears there, in a long grey dress, striped pinafore, a mob cap and black shoes. Apparently, she has been seen to run her finger disapprovingly over the furniture! In 1985, a school party saw her, and she shook her feather duster in a child's face. She has been observed moving about the needlework room, standing in the main bedroom and emerging from the Rupert Room.

In ***Walking in Haunted Gloucestershire*** (p. 18), Jackson and Ottewell report that *'A male employee who knew her (Janet) told of strange and unaccountable happenings. "I always like to put my tools away tidily," he said, "but of course when I'm working they get scattered about a bit. One day I was called away in the middle of a job, but, when I got back, my tools were in apple-pie order. I was puzzled, but now I know that, if I go to tea and leave them about, they'll be in place when I get back." Another time, he was working in the dining room, which is long and rather narrow, when he saw a light passing right down the room. "It looked like a candle being carried," he said. "I couldn't see* *anything but the light. And I watched it pass right down the whole length of the room and through the door at the far end." Perhaps the most eerie happening was one which occurred on a day when the dining room was full of visitors and the waitresses exceptionally busy. One of them carried a heavily laden tray towards the kitchens, but, as she reached the door at the end of the room, two hands appeared in front of her and pushed it open! In her fright she dropped the tray, smashing most of the china on it.'*

North Lodge, Castle Street

The Lodge was built in 1887 by John Oakey. Apparently, many years ago, the couple living there had one little girl whose constant companion was her dog. She was ill for a long time, and when she died the dog pined away. There have been many reports of people hearing the child and the dog playing together and the dog scratching at the door; there has also been one report of a deaf lady seeing the little girl playing with the dog in the house.

"Ye Fayre Ladye of Guytynge Woode"

Frederick Simmons (1828 - 1908), once steward at Sudeley Castle, tells the following story in his notebook of recollections:

"There are several places in our Cotswold Hills, that have the reputation of being haunted spots, and many of the labourers about here would not dare to go alone at night into a region of that repute. The above legend hinges on a story which, some years ago, was 'rhymed and sung' at a 'Blue Ball' at Sudeley Castle, given by the late Earl of Ellenborough in 1832. It was an invitation Ball to Tories of those days.

The story runs as follows:-

The hounds met at 'Guytynge Woode' and a good field of horsemen were at the meet. The Abbot of Hayles was there also, and he espied a 'ladye' mounted on a white horse. A burning desire took possession of him to address her, but all day long he could not get a chance to do so; try how he would, she 'cut him' mysteriously.

At last, the hunt was over, and he saw her riding towards the bottom of the wood, and in the direction in which he was going: he then boldly determined to overtake her, and on doing so, the Abbot looked her in the face, when, to his inexpressible horror, the face was transformed to the Devil with cloven feet!

The Abbot's punishment was a religious one, as no Cleric of the Church in those days dare look at a woman! No doubt the Abbot made the best of his way home!"

Mark Dent Brocklehurst

There are frequent reports from visitors to Sudeley Castle that they can hear someone playing the piano, and, when they reach the library on their tour, they claim to see Mark Dent Brocklehurst seated at the piano. This is apparently a benevolent haunting, and the vibrations they get are happy ones as the former husband of Lady Ashcombe enjoys family time. Visitors say they hear snatches of conversation as he chats to his family. Mark Dent Brocklehurst was a stockbroker who died suddenly from a heart attack in 1972, at the age of 40. By all accounts, he was a devoted family man, a good friend and a storyteller with a brilliant sense of humour.

His sister Katie has reported that, when they were children, one dark and stormy night, two pet poodles suddenly jumped up and barked in a frenzied manner, as their wild eyes followed a passing shadow. The family came to the conclusion that the shadow was one of the castle ghosts.

Lady Elizabeth Ashcombe, Mr Dent Brocklehurst's wife, tells the story of a practical joke he used to play on his mother. Mary Dent Brocklehurst had two spoilt poodles who used to lie next to her when she sat in front of the television of an evening. If she dropped off, Mark would squirt the poodles with a small water pistol, making them jump up and rush around barking furiously. When all was quiet, and Mrs Dent Brocklehurst snoozing once again, he would repeat the performance, while his wife tried hard to suppress her laughter. By the second or third disturbance, their mistress would become suspicious and ask her son if he were doing something to upset them. *"Mark would look up from his paper and say with convincing innocence, 'No Mummy, it must be the ghost again.'"*

THE LION INN

The Lion Inn, formerly ***The White Lion,*** was probably named after the Cotswold Lion, a large breed of sheep with a white face and a long fleece, prized for its heavy wool clip. ***The Lion*** is an old Fifteenth Century coaching inn, built of Cotswold stone; some of the ¼ circle stone segments in the building are thought to have been rescued from the Winchcombe Abbey when it was destroyed in 1539.

In the 1970s and 80s, and almost certainly before that, there were strange things happening in the Lion Inn! Sonny and June Yetman, the innkeepers, lived at the back of the inn where they were never troubled by paranormal activity, but it was a different story for the guests. Strange footsteps disturbed the visitors during the hours of darkness, and, however carefully the door to the Fireplace Room was closed at night, every morning it was open!

There was definitely something strange down in the cellar, as well. Fred Rodgers, the man who did the bottling, always kept everything in apple pie order, but things were moved during the night.

He was not the only one to be aware of something sinister. Scrumpy, the corgi, backed off, growling, whenever the cellar flap was opened, and he almost chewed the flap right through, as if he was trying to stop people going down there.

Who was haunting the inn? Could it have been Jack Slater, who carved his name into the wall of the eaves in 1702?

THE WHITE HART

The White Hart before it was altered by Emma Dent to make it look more quaintly old

The Garden Bar at the back of The White Hart

Another of Winchcombe's old inns, ***The White Hart,*** also has a history of hauntings. Andrew Crump, landlord from 1988 until 1992, tells of a young boy he used to see walking across the back of the Cellar Room, which is now known as the Garden Bar.

He was not the only one to see the boy. A band used to practise in the room and the members of the band, quite independently, also realised that they were not alone.

One day Mr Crump grew annoyed with the apparition and swore at it; he never saw it again. What was the poor boy's story? Nobody seems to know. Mr Crump, however, did find evidence of a fire in the cellar room when they decorated and exposed the charred beams.

There are many reports of more recent hauntings. A member of staff saw someone walking into the Wine and Sausage Bar, but, when she immediately followed, intending to serve the customer, the room was empty. Visitors sometimes report seeing people in their bedrooms and hearing strange noises: one couple even slept in their car recently because they were too scared to stay in the bedroom.

THE CORNER CUPBOARD

"Ye Olde Corner Cupboard" was built in the Sixteenth Century as a farmhouse, using some of the stone from the old Abbey which had been demolished in 1539. It became an inn in 1877.

It is reported that, not long afterwards, a twelve-year old girl who worked at the inn rejected the amorous advances of the landlord. Outraged, he threw her down the stone steps at the back of the inn, killing her.

Customers and staff have reported varying stories, usually involving childish footsteps. They have been heard running the full length of the upstairs, even though there is now a wall half-way across. There have also been fleeting glimpses of a young girl in a long blue dress, usually at the back of the inn. A rocking chair has also been heard moving upstairs.

In ***Walking in Haunted Gloucestershire***, Jackson and Ottewell report learning that a former landlady of the inn laid her collection of Victorian dolls neatly on the bed. She left the room for a few minutes to find, on her return, that the dolls had been thrown untidily all over the bed. Another story involves a barmaid, Gwen, who enjoyed a relaxing glass of cider after work. She found that her drink was deliberately thrown into her lap – but only if she was wearing a blue dress! After her death, some customers claimed to have seen her ghost in the bar.

One incident of haunting at least can be easily explained. One holiday-maker wrote in the Visitor's Book about *"ghostly scratchings in the night"*. The landlady was convinced that this was her cat in his litter tray in the room next door.

'Ye Olde Corner Cupboard', Gloucester Street

Abbey Terrace in the 1930s. Bleby House is in the centre, covered by a creeper.

MORE HAUNTINGS

Bleby House

Bob Meredith, in ***The Haunted Cotswolds,*** tells that a woman dressed like a nun or a nurse haunts Bleby House on Abbey Terrace, often having been seen upstairs. The owners reported several experiences when their young son asked who the kind lady was who sat and talked to him when he was in bed.

In addition to this, there has been a lot of strange activity, as if the house resents intruders. This includes lights being switched on, a radio suddenly starting up, rattling doorknobs, a door being flung open to hit the wall, and things being moved around. Strangest of all happened one night when the occupants felt that the house had been so unpleasant that they locked the bedroom door when they retired for the night. In the early hours, water suddenly started pouring out of the taps in the bedroom washbasin and the dogs were barking frantically downstairs. The taps were turned off securely, but, as soon as the light went off, the water started gushing again. This happened for three nights in succession.

One former resident reported that their cat refused to go down into the cellar, which is all that remains of the original Elizabethan house. In ***Pevsner's Architectural Guide,*** the house is described as having a basement room at the back with *"Sixteenth Century stone archways with keystones and imposts and an exposed foundation stone (which) was clearly part of a moulded column from the Abbey."* It has been suggested that the building was once connected to Winchcombe Abbey by a tunnel, a possibility which might explain the hauntings!

Another haunted house in the town

Bob Meredith tells of another haunting, occurring during 1964-5, on the opposite side of town, in a house with a semi-basement kitchen. One evening, the occupant became aware of a shadow in one corner of the kitchen, which gradually assumed the form of an old woman. She had a thin, pock-marked face and long white hair in plaits, and she was wearing a long, old-fashioned dress made of white lace. Behind her was visible a strange outline of a trench that seemed to run right through the kitchen wall into the bank behind it. Gradually, the image faded. The most distressing things about the sighting were the overwhelming feeling of sadness which weighed upon the occupant and a nauseating smell of rotting flesh.

Puckpit Lane

"We find towns, villages, wells, farms, fields called after (fairies), as in Winchcombe we have Puckpit Lane, and Puckpit fields, and, in Sudeley, at the foot of Humblebee Wood, a beautiful spring of water called Puck's Well. Puck was a ringleader of the fairies, and whether he still haunts those parts which bear his name is not for me to decide; but strange stories are told of strange sights and sounds. Thus one, whose word cannot be doubted, relates how some years ago, having occasion to pass that way during the short hours of the night, he saw a man with a paddle in his hand and a black dog by his side, come noiselessly towards him through the gate which is known as Ham Gate. The road being lonely he hurried on, thinking to join the man for company, but to his surprise he could not overtake him, man and dog always keeping ahead, till they suddenly disappeared. Suspecting something wrong, he retraced his steps, now and again glancing back, when he always saw them following at a short distance, in the same manner as they had preceded him. There was also a strange sound as of stones being thrown after him. On reaching Ham Gate, man

and dog glided noiselessly through the bars of the closed gate! The mysterious dog has since been frequently seen in that locality, and the noise heard of falling stones. Horses sometimes refuse to pass the gate, sometimes stumble or shy. (Curious to relate a horse never fell with me but once, and it was on that very spot that the fall took place). On another occasion my informant saw standing at the gate 'a very respectably dressed man, but with such unmistakeably cloven feet' that he did not dare to linger or investigate but hurried on his way."

Emma Dent's ***'Winchcombe and Sudeley Record**,* May 1882

Winchcombe Railway Tunnel

In ***Folklore and Mysteries of the Cotswolds,*** Mark Turner includes a story told him by a train driver who said that: *"In 1977, when he was a youth of sixteen, he saw an apparition near the mouth of the Winchcombe Railway Tunnel at the Gretton end. ... The four youths were larking around near the tunnel, and as they began walking away, the gentleman giving this report looked back towards the mouth of the tunnel. About twenty yards away and walking towards them, he saw the figure of what he thought was a railwayman wearing cap and working clothes. Intending to tell his friends to run for it, he looked away and then quickly back again. The figure had completely vanished. Yet there was nowhere it could have gone, and in the couple of seconds it took the gentleman to look away the figure could not even have dived to the ground." (pp. 176-7)*

The witness was frightened by this incident, but his friends saw nothing. He recalled that the figure's face was *"very pale and white, with a fixed stare. The figure had been wearing rather old-fashioned working clothes ... though the figure had been walking on the rough stone ballast, it made no sound."* Apparently a railway worker had been killed near the tunnel in the 1920s.

Coscombe Grove

Reverend Lister of Didbrook told Emma Dent about the 'white lady' of Coscombe Grove. She is said to have appeared to many people at the point where the road passes through the wood near the top of Stanway Hill. She is reported to be a servant who lived at Lower Coscombe at the beginning of the 19th Century. She worked at the farm house which had formerly been the country seat of the Abbot of Hailes. She is said to have been murdered and, indeed, the remains of a young woman were discovered in the courtyard when some building works were being carried out.

Winchcombe Police Station

Mark Turner also reports sightings of a young boy at the top of the stairs in the police station in such a position that it would be impossible for a human being to stand. One officer ran up the stairs and felt *"a 'block' of ice-cold air, so distinct that it was possible to walk in and out of it."* The station is now a block of flats, and residents tell of weird and creepy sensations. Pat Smith, who used to keep the garage on the opposite corner from the police station, disinterred a skeleton when he was digging a drain along the front edge of the property. The skeleton was complete except for the left heel, which had presumably been broken off during a previous excavation. He told the police station, but they seemed to think it was a practical joke, so he removed the head and placed it on their counter! It was examined, but nothing was done because it was 'of a certain age'.

Before 1823, people who committed suicide were buried, without religious ceremony and with a stake through their hearts, at a cross roads. This was possibly to confuse the ghost of the deceased, or because executions commonly happened at crossroads, or because that was the nearest lawful resting place to a religious symbol. No wonder there is a lot of paranormal activity at this junction!

BLACK MAGIC

Blizard the Wizard

On 24th January, 1836, Bevil Blizard, *'The Last Necromancer of Winchcombe'*, died at the age of ninety-four. In December 1892, Emma Dent wrote about him in ***The Winchcombe and Sudeley Record:*** *"It was said that he possessed supernatural powers bestowed by the Evil One. He lived alone. Studied magic, 'read the Bible backwards', and was looked upon by his fellow workmen with a certain superstitious awe."*

Once, when he was cutting hay, he suddenly announced that his hen roost was being robbed and quickly set off for home. The other reapers were amazed to see his scythe carry on working by itself! Another time, a Winchcombe man who had been robbed went to Blizard to find out the identity of the thief. The Necromancer told him that he would see the culprit on his way home, where Wickfield Lane crosses the high road. Apparently, when the thief was accused, he confessed on the spot and returned the stolen property.

John Witts also went to him because his scythe had been stolen. Blizard told Witts not to worry because the thief, one Anthony Martin, would never mow again. Blizard told Witts to help himself to an old scythe from his barn, which the wizard then sharpened with a halfpenny until it cut better than any other scythe! Anthony Martin never did mow again, but whether through rheumatism or black magic it is not known.

"Job Washbourne, the father of my (Emma Dent's) *informant, had implicit faith in our magician; but on one occasion this was so severely taxed that he walked straight out of the house for fear of what might happen next. On this dread occasion he was*

invited to join with him in a game of cards. He began by placing nine candles on the table. These 'lighted up of themselves' and then danced about to the utter consternation of poor Job. Nor was this all for after this dance 'they put themselves out', all but two; a pack of cards then appeared on the table ready for use, but by that time Job 'had had enough'."

Blizard lived at Oxenton and was buried in the churchyard there. However, even after his death, his spirit was restless, and local residents frequently saw him, usually at the church gates. *"He was last seen by one Anne Tustin at the Oxenton Church gate; of her witness there can be no doubt as she, good body, was not given to romance."*

Charles Pardington

In his ***'Reminiscences,'*** John Oakey wrote about another man thought to have supernatural powers of detection: *"Another strange character was Charles Pardington, in no way connected with the present family of the same name. He lived in small very old thatched cottage on the Greet Road, a one room cot. He had a quarry on Cleeve Hill which he worked all by himself. He was called the 'Cunning Man', and by some the 'Devil's Man', on account of the uncanny things he did, for he professed to find out thieves and evil doers.*

He was of rather superior education to the ordinary run of his class. In some of these cases he was successful and thus held up his reputation. He even aspired to conduct an evening class in his cottage during the winter. He was killed in 1864 by a fall of rock in his own quarry.

One of his cases occurred almost next door to where I lived (Balloon House, Gloucester Street). *A small shopkeeper, a woman, lost various small sums from her till, so she employed Charles Pardington to find the culprit. Charles secretly questioned her children, of whom she had several, and he also talked to the neighbours and to another shopkeeper. Eventually he fixed it (rightly no doubt) on her eldest daughter. He sought the mother and told her he had found the thief and asked what punishment she wished to inflict on the guilty one. He was to inflict all the curses he was master of, and this he did in his mysterious way with weird signs and mysterious words. He later made known the culprit, who then received a terrible beating.*

After a day and night's reflection, the mother decided that Charles should remove the curses, which he did in the same mysterious manner. Being purged of her sins, the daughter afterwards married and lived to a good age. ... Charles also, to my knowledge, found the thief who stole his mate's tools – again enhancing his reputation." (pp.83-5)

Drawing taken from Emma Dent's ***Record of Winchcombe & Sudeley***

The Witch of Broadwater

In November, 1892, the ***Winchcombe Record*** reported a story by Frederick Simmonds. He, Old Hewins, four beaters and Toby, *'a famous badger dog'* went to Pinnock Wood, hunting a badger. They caught their prey but *"the badger seemed possessed of miraculous power for he bounded away from the dog and ... gave three of the most horrid yells conceivable. I must confess the yells were so unearthly that they fairly made one start, and, what was even more astonishing, Toby dropped to the ground and then slunk back in the greatest fear to his respected master, Hewins."*

To Mr Simmonds' disgust, Old Hewins and the beaters believed that the dog would not have behaved in this way if it had been a real badger. They were convinced that the badger was the devil, and that the place was haunted. On the way back, Old Hewins told the following story: *"My lads, does you recollect that many years ago, there was an ould witch as lived at Broadwater Cottage? ... Well, my opinion is that that there ould 'ooman was along o' we tonight. I very well remembers that a party o' genelmen met just above Broadwater Cottages, as be now in ruins, for a bit o' coursin.*

They had two famous dogs, and they soon started a hare, which made straight for the old cottage as was ockipied by ould Ady Webb. The hare jumped slap in at the window, which was open, and the dogs was so close on her that they scrat her with their tith as her jumped in. Of course the genelmen then went in to find the hare, but the deuce a hare was there! Ould Ady was a-sitting crouched over the fire and blood was runnin' down her arm. The genelmen walked off pretty sharp, I can tell 'ee.

Then I can tell 'ee summat else about the ould 'ooman. ... her once gin Bill Smith, of Guiting, a nice black cat, an put him in a basket, an tied him in with a piece o' string. So off Willum started whoam with 'un, and when he got to Wainstone Gate he thought he 'ood look at 'un, and I'm blowed if he wasn't gone, and the string 'ad never bin untied!

Bless 'ee, I could keep on telling 'ee no end o' things about her; her had dealings with the powers o' darkness, there yunt the least doubt. Why, when Edward Webb went a hay carring, in a field close to Broadwater, ould Ady come out o' her house and axed him for some drink, an he 'oodn't gie her none, an when they began loadin up the hay it kept slippin off as fast as ever they put it on. They tried five times, and then gin out and went whoam, and their measter telled 'em to allus for the future give ould Ady anything her axed for, and they allus did arter, and then they had good fortin.

I'll tell 'ee one more thing as her done and then I think you'll all be convinced what her wus. You knows there be stepping stoans thro' the brook at Broadwater, ... Well then, a man by the name o' Jim Hardyman come down to the brook one day, an ould Ady was a standin at her door. Her called out to he not to walk across the stepping stoans, but he 'ood persist and as soon as ever he trod on the fust, down he goes right slap into the brook; and there he lay, an couldn't get up, till he begged ould Ady to come an help him.

Now I think this is quite enough to convince any on 'ee that that place wus really haunted, an arter what we a sin and heard tonight, I've no doubt in my mind but what ould Ady wus in that there badger."

More local witches

"Tales are told how horses have been ill-treated by witches; found 'all of a sweat' in the morning with tangled mane and tail, showing how they must have been ridden during the night. Consequently horse shoes are hung as charms over the stable doors to break spells and protect the animals. According to another report, a witch or white lady appears in a neighbouring wood, haunting the road, alarming the carters' horses, so that they tremble and foam from fright, and in spite of word and whip utterly refuse to go on.

Mr C. Stewart of Gloucester Street, who narrated the above as a well known and authenticated fact, is a carpenter, and on being asked whether he had ever seen or heard anything of this supernatural being, replied emphatically in the negative. But then he added, by way of explanation: 'In the course of my business I have had frequent occasion to pass through the wood, by the haunted road, bearing a coffin to the house of death. Now there is such superstitious dread of meeting anyone with a coffin, that I have known and seen people fly over hedge and ditch to avoid me, and so I imagine that the coffin acted as a charm in keeping off the evil and mysterious spirit."

Winchcombe and Sudeley Record, Sept. 1892

In October 1892, Mrs Dent recorded some local stories about "*the power of the evil eye, and of the way in which witches could arrest horses, teams, etc. By Stumps' Cross Pike and half way up on Stanway Hill, horses shy, stand stock still, and otherwise show signs of uneasiness. The same took place on the Gretton Road by 'Margrett's Stream'. Fisher, a labourer living in Tythe Court, tells how, years ago when turnpikes were on the roads, it used to be the practice of farmers and others, sending teams to Tewkesbury, to start soon after 12 o'clock at night so as to save double toll. One night, whilst going along the Gretton Road, he (Fisher) was riding the foremost horse, when an apparition, clothed in white, came swiftly by them and so startled the horse that it jumped clean from under him, and, of course, down came Master Fisher. His master, who was with the team, saw the figure at the same time, and the horses were so scared that it was with the greatest difficulty they could make them proceed."*

Another story was told to her by the Clerk at Didbrook who remembered his father telling him of a witch who lived in a house at the end of the village. Apparently, she used to cast a spell to make horses balk at the stream. One particular carter was so annoyed by frequently having this spell cast on his horses that he went to the old woman's house, engaged her in conversation and then struck her with a whip, making sure that he drew blood. As soon as this happened, the horses set off at the gallop.

Torchlight funeral

Emma Dent explains that the reason for placing lighted candles near the dead was to scare off witches or evil spirits, and for this reason some funerals used to be held at night. The last funeral by torch-light in Winchcombe was that of Mrs Elizabeth Innell who was buried on October 23rd, 1831. Mr Edwin Johnson of Hailes Street witnessed her funeral as a young boy and described it to Mrs Dent. *"The awful solemnity of the occasion was increased tenfold by those trappings of woe, now, happily, nearly extinct, viz. mutes in ghastly array standing as sentinels, staves in hand, emblems of death, on either side the entrance gate; pall bearers and mourners wearing long-flowing hat bands and scarves. The night was pitch dark, but the numerous torches fixed on poles threw lurid and fitful lights in that chill October night on the gloomy procession which moved slowly and solemnly from the Abbey grounds, amid a large concourse of people, who preserved during the whole of the ceremony profound silence and great decorum."*

The Winchcombe Imp

"As the devil endeavoured, according to the legend, to frustrate the building of the great Cathedral at Lincoln, so he did, it is said, all he could to prevent the parishioners of Winchcombe from erecting their parish church, but,

The Christians of those troublous years
Were steadfast, brave, and true:
They fought the devil with their might,
Until away he flew.

They carved his ugly face in wood,
And nailed it to the screen;
And there the cunning, grinning imp
May to this day be seen.

Verse by Rev. T.E. Meurig Davies

THE ORIGINS OF SOME GHOST STORIES

Deliberate Deception

Scaring People Away - John Oakey tells that body-snatching was frequent in Winchcombe. Body-snatchers, or 'Resurrectionists', were employed by anatomists to provide recently deceased corpses for anatomical research. They would tell stories of hauntings in churchyards to frighten people away while they dug up the bodies. In 1832, the Anatomy Act was passed allowing anatomists access to the workhouse dead; before then only the bodies of executed murderers could legally be dissected.

A 19th C. cartoon of bodysnatchers

Emma Dent gives a different explanation for stories of a haunted churchyard in the ***Record*** of October 1891. She reports that *"here in Winchcombe ... many have been the ghostly tales of sights and sounds and shadows connected with her churchyard. 'Body-snatching', we know, was only a few years ago a not uncommon practice. To check this it was a matter of expediency to encourage a belief in churchyard gloom and midnight horrors."*

Giving a Thrill - In ***A Cotswold Ragbag,*** Bert Butler recalls that he was an under-gardener at Sudeley Castle in August 1928, when a thousand men of the Royal Warwickshire Regiment were camped on the estate: *"Those lads constantly gave us 'Woodbines'* (cigarettes) *and were soon asking us to show them the 'Haunted Door'. Some clever-dick back in camp had told them on no account to miss seeing it. While eating our bait the next morning, I told Frank that the soldier lads positively needed a good ghost story to complete their pleasure in Sudeley Castle. A real snorter of a story to tell the folk at home.*

So there and then we made up a beauty! We gave them good value for Woodbines, with headless knights in armour, rattling chains, Sudeley's version of the Hound of the Baskervilles, horrible screams that rose to a terrifying crescendo at midnight at the full moon. Frank and I were chaps who did our work properly, so we made a good job of this one, and, for good measure, threw in the ghost of a grey-gowned nun, who also chose full-moon night to arise from the icy water of the moat. We rehearsed the rigmarole a bit, so that we should tell (more or less) the same story. We always ended by telling the lads that we had never seen or heard anything ***ourselves,*** *implying that others may have seen the whole show!"*

Misinterpreting Natural Phenomena

Margrett's Stream Hollow (see pp.86-7) - Emma Dent records that the mystery of was solved when one brave man challenged the *'nightly visitor'*. He found that *"this most alarming 'ghost' was nothing more than an inoffensive cow of the Hereford tribe, whose snow-white face was clearly visible to the naked eye."*

Frederick Simmons tells another interesting tale in his ***Memories***:

'A Mystery of Limehill Barn on Sudeley Estate'

'About the year 1838, certain repairs and alterations were carried out at Limehill Barn (near Spoonley Wood), and, in digging for gravel & sand in the yard close to the old barn, the men employed came upon a human skull, and, carefully uncovering the skeleton, discovered that the body must have been put into the ground in a limp state, as the body was bent to the feet (skull and feet together). This made the workmen believe that a murder had been committed there, and a great awe took possession of them, especially towards the approach of night!

Now, some years after, I had to go to Limehill Wood to hunt a badger, and I took with me one of the men that had worked at the barn above-mentioned. He was as brave at anything 'human' as I could have wished, and his name was Jim. I sent Jim round with scouting dogs to disturb the badger and force him to run for his earth, where I was waiting with a couple of bull terriers. I had been expecting to hear my 'huntsman' encouraging his dogs, but not a sound could I hear for half an hour. At last I heard a great rushing through the bush, and Jim appeared – white in the face with terror – exclaiming, "Master, this place is haunted."

The time was midnight and a bright moon looking down.
I exclaimed, "Jim, don't be a fool!"
He replied, "I be no fool! I've heard some dreadful sounds, Master! There's a sperit about!" I began to wax wroth with him, and he said, "Oh Master, don't you remember me digging out that skelenton at the barn down yonder?"
I said, "What the deuce has that got to do with it?"
He replied, "A good deal! I'm off! I can do with what I can see, but them there sounds be'ant made by we. 'Tis a warning, and it's the sperit of that 'ooman that was murdered in the barn."
I listened and certainly could hear mysterious groans on the hill.
I said to Jim, "It's a bird, that's all."
He replied, "Oh Master, it's no bird! Let they stop as will – my name's Walker!" To my annoyance, every one of the fellows (4 of them) decamped for home! Of course, I had to give up the hunt and I followed them, not in an agreeable temper.

Now I determined next evening to thrash out this mystery, so I took my gun and cartridges and went to this secluded spot where the sounds came from, called the 'Diamond plantation'. I arrived there at about 5 o'clock on a November evening. It was twilight. Believing it was a bird of some sort, I fixed my eyes at the top of the trees, skyward. At last, a dark bird of large size alighted on a tree. I fired and dropped him. In a few moments another came and I killed it. It was now so dark that I could not see them on the ground, so I lit a march and, by the light, found them and made for home. On taking them out of my pocket, I was greatly surprised to find they were Horned Owls, which accounted for the strange moanings which poor Jim heard. They make a moaning cry, almost, you might fancy, a despairing wail for something lost for ever!"

Accidental Incidents

The Ghost Bells - This story was told by Eddie Febry in ***Winchcombe: Our Home – Our Heritage, A Celebration of the Millenium:***
One day in 1948, the Vicar of St. Peter's Church went to Almsbury Farm and asked the farmer, Jim Hitch, for help with getting rid of pigeons in the belfry. Eddy and Mike, another worker went to the Church that night. *"Armed with torch and rifle, we climbed the stone steps to the belfry. As we climbed the narrow winding steps, I had a funny feeling in my stomach, and then I heard this noise. We both stopped dead. There was this terrible grinding and groaning, then the clock struck the quarter. My hair was on end, and I was almost dropping messages of love with the pigeons. Mike said, "Come on," and reached the belfry. I held the torch; Mike shot the pigeons. In the process, a number of pellets hit the bells, making them ring softly. Two or three days later, a tent appeared in the churchyard. Mr Basset Green from Basset House, Gretton Road, who was the local ghost hunter, was waiting to hear the ghost bells that had been reported!"*

Bibliography

Books:

Ashcombe, E. (2009) ***Behind Castle Walls,*** Amberley Publishing
Brooks, J.A. (1986) ***Ghosts and Witches of the Cotswolds,*** Jarrold
Butler, B. (1984) ***A Cotswold Rag-Bag,*** Sue Ryder Foundation
Darby, N. (2009) ***Foul Deeds and Suspicious Deaths in the Cotswolds,*** Pen and Sword Books Ltd.
Dent, E. (1877) ***Annals of Winchcombe and Sudeley,*** John Murray
Dent, E. (1890s) ***The Winchcombe and Sudeley Record***
Donaldson, D.N. (2001) ***Winchcombe,*** Wychwood Press
Jackson, F. E. & Ottewell, G. (1994) ***Walking in Haunted Gloucestershire,*** Sigma Leisure
Meredith, B. (1990) ***The Haunted Cotswolds,*** Reardon and Son
Oakey, J. (2014) ***Reminiscences,*** Winchcombe Town Trust
Palmer, R. (1994) ***Folklore of Gloucestershire,*** Tempus
Simmons, F. ***Memoirs and Memories,*** Winchcombe Museum
Stevinson, J. (2005) ***King Kenulf and St Kenelm,*** St. Peter's Church
The People of Winchcombe (2000) ***Winchcombe: Our Home – Our Heritage, A Celebration of the Millenium,*** Quorum T.S. Ltd.
Turner, M. (1993) ***Folklore and Mysteries of the Cotswolds,*** Robert Hale
Verey, D. and Brooks, A. (1999) ***Pevsner Architectural Guides,*** Yale

Websites:

http://www.hedgedruid.com/tag/belas-knap/
http://www.haunted-britain.com/corner-cupboard-inn.htm

Winchcombe

Folk & Police

Museum

All profits from this publication will go to ***Winchcombe Folk and Police Museum,*** part of The Winchcombe Town Trust, registered charity no. 234734.

The Museum is staffed entirely by volunteers. We do not only look after a fascinating collection of objects and pictures, spanning the history of Winchcombe from the Stone Age to the Twentieth Century; we also guide visitors round the Museum and answer their questions about the town. We help visitors to research their family history, and we do our own research into interesting aspects of Winchcombe's heritage, which we then put into folders that visitors can browse through. And, of course, we publish books like this one to raise money for the museum!

If any of these activities interest you, please come along and have a look around. We welcome new volunteers to our friendly team. You will find us in the centre of town, at the Old Town Hall, next to the Tourist Information Centre. We are open from 1st April until 31st October, Monday to Saturday, from ten o'clock until four.

ACCREDITED MUSEUM

'Murder Alley', Hailes Street, the site of the murder of Louisa Bingham, 1904